Dream Psychology: Psychoanalysis for Beginners

Sigmund Freud

THE MILKY WAY
PUBLICATIONS

ISBN: 978-81-991983-5-7

Publisher: The Milky Way Publications
Mumbai, Maharashtra

Phone: +91 916708046
WhatsApp: +91 9167080479
E-mail: themilkywaypublications@gmail.com

First Edition: 2025

Dream Psychology: Psychoanalysis for Beginners
Sigmund Freud

CONTENTS

I. DREAMS HAVE A MEANING 11

II. THE DREAM MECHANISM 25

III. WHY THE DREAM DISGUISES THE DESIRES 44

IV. DREAM ANALYSIS 56

V. SEX IN DREAMS 71

VI. THE WISH IN DREAMS 89

VII. THE FUNCTION OF THE DREAM 106

VIII. THE PRIMARY AND SECONDARY PROCESS–REGRESSION 119

IX. THE UNCONSCIOUS AND CONSCIOUSNESS–REALITY 140

INTRODUCTION

The medical profession is justly conservative. Human life should not be considered as the proper material for wild experiments.

Conservatism, however, is too often a welcome excuse for lazy minds, loath to adapt themselves to fast changing conditions.

Remember the scornful reception which first was accorded to Freud's discoveries in the domain of the unconscious.

When after years of patient observations, he finally decided to appear before medical bodies to tell them modestly of some facts which always recurred in his dream and his patients' dreams, he was first laughed at and then avoided as a crank.

The words "dream interpretation" were and still are indeed fraught with unpleasant, unscientific associations. They remind one of all sorts of childish, superstitious notions, which make up the thread and woof of dream books, read by none but the ignorant and the primitive.

The wealth of detail, the infinite care never to let anything pass unexplained, with which he presented to the public the result of his investigations, are impressing more and more serious-minded scientists, but the examination of his evidential data demands arduous work and presupposes an absolutely open mind.

This is why we still encounter men, totally unfamiliar with Freud's writings, men who were not even interested enough in the subject to attempt an interpretation of their dreams or their patients' dreams, deriding Freud's theories and combatting them with the help of

statements which he never made.

Some of them, like Professor Boris Sidis, reach at times conclusions which are strangely similar to Freud's, but in their ignorance of psychoanalytic literature, they fail to credit Freud for observations antedating theirs.

Besides those who sneer at dream study, because they have never looked into the subject, there are those who do not dare to face the facts revealed by dream study. Dreams tell us many an unpleasant biological truth about ourselves and only very free minds can thrive on such a diet. Self-deception is a plant which withers fast in the pellucid atmosphere of dream investigation.

The weakling and the neurotic attached to his neurosis are not anxious to turn such a powerful searchlight upon the dark corners of their psychology.

Freud's theories are anything but theoretical.

He was moved by the fact that there always seemed to be a close connection between his patients' dreams and their mental abnormalities, to collect thousands of dreams and to compare them with the case histories in his possession.

He did not start out with a preconceived bias, hoping to find evidence which might support his views. He looked at facts a thousand times "until they began to tell him something."

His attitude toward dream study was, in other words, that of a statistician who does not know, and has no means of foreseeing, what conclusions will be forced on him by the information he is gathering, but who is fully prepared to accept those unavoidable conclusions.

This was indeed a novel way in psychology. Psychologists had always been wont to build, in what Bleuler calls "autistic ways," that is through methods in no wise supported by evidence, some attractive hypothesis, which sprung from their brain, like Minerva from Jove's brain, fully armed.

After which, they would stretch upon that unyielding frame the hide of a reality which they had previously killed.

It is only to minds suffering from the same distortions, to minds also autistically inclined, that those empty, artificial structures appear acceptable molds for philosophic thinking.

The pragmatic view that "truth is what works" had not been as yet expressed when Freud published his revolutionary views on the psychology of dreams.

Five facts of first magnitude were made obvious to the world by his interpretation of dreams.

First of all, Freud pointed out a constant connection between some part of every dream and some detail of the dreamer's life during the previous waking state. This positively establishes a relation between sleeping states and waking states and disposes of the widely prevalent view that dreams are purely nonsensical phenomena coming from nowhere and leading nowhere.

Secondly, Freud, after studying the dreamer's life and modes of thought, after noting down all his mannerisms and the apparently insignificant details of his conduct which reveal his secret thoughts, came to the conclusion that there was in every dream the attempted or successful gratification of some wish, conscious or unconscious.

Thirdly, he proved that many of our dream visions are symbolical, which causes us to consider them as absurd and unintelligible; the universality of those symbols, however, makes them very transparent to the trained observer.

Fourthly, Freud showed that sexual desires play an enormous part in our unconscious, a part which puritanical hypocrisy has always tried to minimize, if not to ignore entirely.

Finally, Freud established a direct connection between dreams and insanity, between the symbolic visions of our sleep and the symbolic actions of the mentally deranged.

There were, of course, many other observations which Freud made while dissecting the dreams of his patients, but not all of them present

as much interest as the foregoing nor were they as revolutionary or likely to wield as much influence on modern psychiatry.

Other explorers have struck the path blazed by Freud and leading into man's unconscious. Jung of Zurich, Adler of Vienna and Kempf of Washington, D.C., have made to the study of the unconscious, contributions which have brought that study into fields which Freud himself never dreamt of invading.

One fact which cannot be too emphatically stated, however, is that but for Freud's wishfulfillment theory of dreams, neither Jung's "energic theory," nor Adler's theory of "organ inferiority and compensation," nor Kempf's "dynamic mechanism" might have been formulated.

Freud is the father of modern abnormal psychology and he established the psychoanalytical point of view. No one who is not well grounded in Freudian lore can hope to achieve any work of value in the field of psychoanalysis.

On the other hand, let no one repeat the absurd assertion that Freudism is a sort of religion bounded with dogmas and requiring an act of faith. Freudism as such was merely a stage in the development of psychoanalysis, a stage out of which all but a few bigoted camp followers, totally lacking in originality, have evolved. Thousands of stones have been added to the structure erected by the Viennese physician and many more will be added in the course of time.

But the new additions to that structure would collapse like a house of cards but for the original foundations which are as indestructible as Harvey's statement as to the circulation of the blood.

Regardless of whatever additions or changes have been made to the original structure, the analytic point of view remains unchanged.

That point of view is not only revolutionising all the methods of diagnosis and treatment of mental derangements, but compelling the intelligent, up-to-date physician to revise entirely his attitude to almost every kind of disease.

The insane are no longer absurd and pitiable people, to be herded in asylums till nature either cures them or relieves them, through death, of their misery. The insane who have not been made so by actual injury to their brain or nervous system, are the victims of unconscious forces which cause them to do abnormally things which they might be helped to do normally.

Insight into one's psychology is replacing victoriously sedatives and rest cures.

Physicians dealing with "purely" physical cases have begun to take into serious consideration the "mental" factors which have predisposed a patient to certain ailments.

Freud's views have also made a revision of all ethical and social values unavoidable and have thrown an unexpected flood of light upon literary and artistic accomplishment.

But the Freudian point of view, or more broadly speaking, the psychoanalytic point of view, shall ever remain a puzzle to those who, from laziness or indifference, refuse to survey with the great Viennese the field over which he carefully groped his way. We shall never be convinced until we repeat under his guidance all his laboratory experiments.

We must follow him through the thickets of the unconscious, through the land which had never been charted because academic philosophers, following the line of least effort, had decided *a priori* that it could not be charted.

Ancient geographers, when exhausting their store of information about distant lands, yielded to an unscientific craving for romance and, without any evidence to support their day dreams, filled the blank spaces left on their maps by unexplored tracts with amusing inserts such as "Here there are lions."

Thanks to Freud's interpretation of dreams the "royal road" into the unconscious is now open to all explorers. They shall not find lions, they shall find man himself, and the record of all his life and of his struggle with reality.

And it is only after seeing man as his unconscious, revealed by his

dreams, presents him to us that we shall understand him fully. For as Freud said to Putnam: "We are what we are because we have been what we have been."

Not a few serious-minded students, however, have been discouraged from attempting a study of Freud's dream psychology.

The book in which he originally offered to the world his interpretation of dreams was as circumstantial as a legal record to be pondered over by scientists at their leisure, not to be assimilated in a few hours by the average alert reader. In those days, Freud could not leave out any detail likely to make his extremely novel thesis evidentially acceptable to those willing to sift data.

Freud himself, however, realized the magnitude of the task which the reading of his *magnum opus* imposed upon those who have not been prepared for it by long psychological and scientific training and he abstracted from that gigantic work the parts which constitute the essential of his discoveries.

The publishers of the present book deserve credit for presenting to the reading public the gist of Freud's psychology in the master's own words, and in a form which shall neither discourage beginners, nor appear too elementary to those who are more advanced in psychoanalytic study.

Dream psychology is the key to Freud's works and to all modern psychology. With a simple, compact manual such as *Dream Psychology* there shall be no longer any excuse for ignorance of the most revolutionary psychological system of modern times.

ANDRE TRIDON.

121 Madison Avenue, New York.

November, 1920.

I

DREAMS HAVE A MEANING

In what we may term "prescientific days" people were in no uncertainty about the interpretation of dreams. When they were recalled after awakening they were regarded as either the friendly or hostile manifestation of some higher powers, demoniacal and Divine. With the rise of scientific thought the whole of this expressive mythology was transferred to psychology; to-day there is but a small minority among educated persons who doubt that the dream is the dreamer's own psychical act.

But since the downfall of the mythological hypothesis an interpretation of the dream has been wanting. The conditions of its origin; its relationship to our psychical life when we are awake; its independence of disturbances which, during the state of sleep, seem to compel notice; its many peculiarities repugnant to our waking thought; the incongruence between its images and the feelings they engender; then the dream's evanescence, the way in which, on awakening, our thoughts thrust it aside as something bizarre, and our reminiscences mutilating or rejecting it—all these and many other problems have for many hundred years demanded answers which up till now could never have been satisfactory. Before all there is the question as to the meaning of the dream, a question which is in itself double-sided. There is, firstly, the psychical significance of the dream, its position with regard to the psychical processes, as to a possible biological function; secondly, has the dream a meaning—can sense be made of each single dream as of other mental syntheses?

Three tendencies can be observed in the estimation of dreams. Many philosophers have given currency to one of these tendencies, one which at the same time preserves something of the dream's former over-valuation. The foundation of dream life is for them a peculiar state of psychical activity, which they even celebrate as elevation to some higher state. Schubert, for instance, claims: "The dream is the liberation of the spirit from the pressure of external nature, a detachment of the soul from the fetters of matter." Not all go so far as this, but many maintain that dreams have their origin in real spiritual excitations, and are the outward manifestations of spiritual powers whose free movements have been hampered during the day ("Dream Phantasies," Scherner, Volkelt). A large number of observers acknowledge that dream life is capable of extraordinary achievements–at any rate, in certain fields ("Memory").

In striking contradiction with this the majority of medical writers hardly admit that the dream is a psychical phenomenon at all. According to them dreams are provoked and initiated exclusively by stimuli proceeding from the senses or the body, which either reach the sleeper from without or are accidental disturbances of his internal organs. The dream has no greater claim to meaning and importance than the sound called forth by the ten fingers of a person quite unacquainted with music running his fingers over the keys of an instrument. The dream is to be regarded, says Binz, "as a physical process always useless, frequently morbid." All the peculiarities of dream life are explicable as the incoherent effort, due to some physiological stimulus, of certain organs, or of the cortical elements of a brain otherwise asleep.

But slightly affected by scientific opinion and untroubled as to the origin of dreams, the popular view holds firmly to the belief that dreams really have got a meaning, in some way they do foretell the future, whilst the meaning can be unravelled in some way or other from its oft bizarre and enigmatical content. The reading of dreams consists in replacing the events of the dream, so far as remembered, by other events. This is done either scene by scene, *according to some rigid key*, or the dream as a whole is replaced by something else of which it was a *symbol*. Serious-minded persons laugh at these efforts–"Dreams are but sea-foam!"

One day I discovered to my amazement that the popular view grounded in superstition, and not the medical one, comes nearer to the truth about dreams. I arrived at new conclusions about dreams by the use of a new method of psychological investigation, one which had rendered me good service in the investigation of phobias, obsessions, illusions, and the like, and which, under the name "psycho-analysis," had found acceptance by a whole school of investigators. The manifold analogies of dream life with the most diverse conditions of psychical disease in the waking state have been rightly insisted upon by a number of medical observers. It seemed, therefore, *a priori*, hopeful to apply to the interpretation of dreams methods of investigation which had been tested in psychopathological processes. Obsessions and those peculiar sensations of haunting dread remain as strange to normal consciousness as do dreams to our waking consciousness; their origin is as unknown to consciousness as is that of dreams. It was practical ends that impelled us, in these diseases, to fathom their origin and formation. Experience had shown us that a cure and a consequent mastery of the obsessing ideas did result when once those thoughts, the connecting links between the morbid ideas and the rest of the psychical content, were revealed which were heretofore veiled from consciousness. The procedure I employed for the interpretation of dreams thus arose from psychotherapy.

This procedure is readily described, although its practice demands instruction and experience. Suppose the patient is suffering from intense morbid dread. He is requested to direct his attention to the idea in question, without, however, as he has so frequently done, meditating upon it. Every impression about it, without any exception, which occurs to him should be imparted to the doctor. The statement which will be perhaps then made, that he cannot concentrate his attention upon anything at all, is to be countered by assuring him most positively that such a blank state of mind is utterly impossible. As a matter of fact, a great number of impressions will soon occur, with which others will associate themselves. These will be invariably accompanied by the expression of the observer's opinion that they have no meaning

or are unimportant. It will be at once noticed that it is this self-criticism which prevented the patient from imparting the ideas, which had indeed already excluded them from consciousness. If the patient can be induced to abandon this self-criticism and to pursue the trains of thought which are yielded by concentrating the attention, most significant matter will be obtained, matter which will be presently seen to be clearly linked to the morbid idea in question. Its connection with other ideas will be manifest, and later on will permit the replacement of the morbid idea by a fresh one, which is perfectly adapted to psychical continuity.

This is not the place to examine thoroughly the hypothesis upon which this experiment rests, or the deductions which follow from its invariable success. It must suffice to state that we obtain matter enough for the resolution of every morbid idea if we especially direct our attention to the *unbidden* associations *which disturb our thoughts*—those which are otherwise put aside by the critic as worthless refuse. If the procedure is exercised on oneself, the best plan of helping the experiment is to write down at once all one's first indistinct fancies.

I will now point out where this method leads when I apply it to the examination of dreams. Any dream could be made use of in this way. From certain motives I, however, choose a dream of my own, which appears confused and meaningless to my memory, and one which has the advantage of brevity. Probably my dream of last night satisfies the requirements. Its content, fixed immediately after awakening, runs as follows:

"*Company; at table or table d'hôte.... Spinach is served. Mrs. E.L., sitting next to me, gives me her undivided attention, and places her hand familiarly upon my knee. In defence I remove her hand. Then she says: 'But you have always had such beautiful eyes.'.... I then distinctly see something like two eyes as a sketch or as the contour of a spectacle lens....*"

This is the whole dream, or, at all events, all that I can remember. It appears to me not only obscure and meaningless, but more especially odd. Mrs. E.L. is a person with whom I am scarcely on

visiting terms, nor to my knowledge have I ever desired any more cordial relationship. I have not seen her for a long time, and do not think there was any mention of her recently. No emotion whatever accompanied the dream process.

Reflecting upon this dream does not make it a bit clearer to my mind. I will now, however, present the ideas, without premeditation and without criticism, which introspection yielded. I soon notice that it is an advantage to break up the dream into its elements, and to search out the ideas which link themselves to each fragment.

Company; at table or table d'hôte. The recollection of the slight event with which the evening of yesterday ended is at once called up. I left a small party in the company of a friend, who offered to drive me home in his cab. "I prefer a taxi," he said; "that gives one such a pleasant occupation; there is always something to look at." When we were in the cab, and the cab-driver turned the disc so that the first sixty hellers were visible, I continued the jest. "We have hardly got in and we already owe sixty hellers. The taxi always reminds me of the table d'hôte. It makes me avaricious and selfish by continuously reminding me of my debt. It seems to me to mount up too quickly, and I am always afraid that I shall be at a disadvantage, just as I cannot resist at table d'hôte the comical fear that I am getting too little, that I must look after myself." In far-fetched connection with this I quote:

"To earth, this weary earth, ye bring us,
To guilt ye let us heedless go."

Another idea about the table d'hôte. A few weeks ago I was very cross with my dear wife at the dinner-table at a Tyrolese health resort, because she was not sufficiently reserved with some neighbors with whom I wished to have absolutely nothing to do. I begged her to occupy herself rather with me than with the strangers. That is just as if I had *been at a disadvantage at the table d'hôte.* The contrast between the behavior of my wife at the table and that of Mrs. E.L. in the dream now strikes me: "*Addresses herself entirely to me.*"

Further, I now notice that the dream is the reproduction of a little scene which transpired between my wife and myself when I was secretly courting her. The caressing under cover of the tablecloth was an answer to a wooer's passionate letter. In the dream, however, my wife is replaced by the unfamiliar E.L.

Mrs. E.L. is the daughter of a man to whom I *owed money*! I cannot help noticing that here there is revealed an unsuspected connection between the dream content and my thoughts. If the chain of associations be followed up which proceeds from one element of the dream one is soon led back to another of its elements. The thoughts evoked by the dream stir up associations which were not noticeable in the dream itself.

Is it not customary, when some one expects others to look after his interests without any advantage to themselves, to ask the innocent question satirically: "Do you think this will be done *for the sake of your beautiful eyes*?" Hence Mrs. E.L.'s speech in the dream. "You have always had such beautiful eyes," means nothing but "people always do everything to you for love of you; you have had *everything for nothing*." The contrary is, of course, the truth; I have always paid dearly for whatever kindness others have shown me. Still, the fact that *I had a ride for nothing* yesterday when my friend drove me home in his cab must have made an impression upon me.

In any case, the friend whose guests we were yesterday has often made me his debtor. Recently I allowed an opportunity of requiting him to go by. He has had only one present from me, an antique shawl, upon which eyes are painted all round, a so-called Occhiale, as a *charm* against the *Malocchio*. Moreover, he is an *eye specialist*. That same evening I had asked him after a patient whom I had sent to him for *glasses*.

As I remarked, nearly all parts of the dream have been brought into this new connection. I still might ask why in the dream it was *spinach* that was served up. Because spinach called up a little scene which recently occurred at our table. A child, whose *beautiful eyes* are really deserving of praise, refused to eat spinach. As a child I was just the same; for a long time I loathed *spinach*, until in later life my tastes

altered, and it became one of my favorite dishes. The mention of this dish brings my own childhood and that of my child's near together. "You should be glad that you have some spinach," his mother had said to the little gourmet. "Some children would be very glad to get spinach." Thus I am reminded of the parents' duties towards their children. Goethe's words–

> "To earth, this weary earth, ye bring us,
> To guilt ye let us heedless go"–

take on another meaning in this connection.

Here I will stop in order that I may recapitulate the results of the analysis of the dream. By following the associations which were linked to the single elements of the dream torn from their context, I have been led to a series of thoughts and reminiscences where I am bound to recognize interesting expressions of my psychical life. The matter yielded by an analysis of the dream stands in intimate relationship with the dream content, but this relationship is so special that I should never have been able to have inferred the new discoveries directly from the dream itself. The dream was passionless, disconnected, and unintelligible. During the time that I am unfolding the thoughts at the back of the dream I feel intense and well-grounded emotions. The thoughts themselves fit beautifully together into chains logically bound together with certain central ideas which ever repeat themselves. Such ideas not represented in the dream itself are in this instance the antitheses *selfish, unselfish, to be indebted, to work for nothing*. I could draw closer the threads of the web which analysis has disclosed, and would then be able to show how they all run together into a single knot; I am debarred from making this work public by considerations of a private, not of a scientific, nature. After having cleared up many things which I do not willingly acknowledge as mine, I should have much to reveal which had better remain my secret. Why, then, do not I choose another dream whose analysis would be more suitable for publication, so that I could awaken a fairer conviction of the sense and cohesion of the results disclosed by analysis? The answer is, because every dream which I investigate

leads to the same difficulties and places me under the same need of discretion; nor should I forgo this difficulty any the more were I to analyze the dream of some one else. That could only be done when opportunity allowed all concealment to be dropped without injury to those who trusted me.

The conclusion which is now forced upon me is that the dream is a *sort of substitution* for those emotional and intellectual trains of thought which I attained after complete analysis. I do not yet know the process by which the dream arose from those thoughts, but I perceive that it is wrong to regard the dream as psychically unimportant, a purely physical process which has arisen from the activity of isolated cortical elements awakened out of sleep.

I must further remark that the dream is far shorter than the thoughts which I hold it replaces; whilst analysis discovered that the dream was provoked by an unimportant occurrence the evening before the dream.

Naturally, I would not draw such far-reaching conclusions if only one analysis were known to me. Experience has shown me that when the associations of any dream are honestly followed such a chain of thought is revealed, the constituent parts of the dream reappear correctly and sensibly linked together; the slight suspicion that this concatenation was merely an accident of a single first observation must, therefore, be absolutely relinquished. I regard it, therefore, as my right to establish this new view by a proper nomenclature. I contrast the dream which my memory evokes with the dream and other added matter revealed by analysis: the former I call the dream's *manifest content*; the latter, without at first further subdivision, its *latent content.* I arrive at two new problems hitherto unformulated: (1) What is the psychical process which has transformed the latent content of the dream into its manifest content? (2) What is the motive or the motives which have made such transformation exigent? The process by which the change from latent to manifest content is executed I name the *dream-work*. In contrast with this is the *work of analysis*, which produces the reverse

transformation. The other problems of the dream—the inquiry as to its stimuli, as to the source of its materials, as to its possible purpose, the function of dreaming, the forgetting of dreams—these I will discuss in connection with the latent dream-content.

I shall take every care to avoid a confusion between the *manifest* and the *latent content*, for I ascribe all the contradictory as well as the incorrect accounts of dream-life to the ignorance of this latent content, now first laid bare through analysis.

The conversion of the latent dream thoughts into those manifest deserves our close study as the first known example of the transformation of psychical stuff from one mode of expression into another. From a mode of expression which, moreover, is readily intelligible into another which we can only penetrate by effort and with guidance, although this new mode must be equally reckoned as an effort of our own psychical activity. From the standpoint of the relationship of latent to manifest dream-content, dreams can be divided into three classes. We can, in the first place, distinguish those dreams which have a *meaning* and are, at the same time, *intelligible*, which allow us to penetrate into our psychical life without further ado. Such dreams are numerous; they are usually short, and, as a general rule, do not seem very noticeable, because everything remarkable or exciting surprise is absent. Their occurrence is, moreover, a strong argument against the doctrine which derives the dream from the isolated activity of certain cortical elements. All signs of a lowered or subdivided psychical activity are wanting. Yet we never raise any objection to characterizing them as dreams, nor do we confound them with the products of our waking life.

A second group is formed by those dreams which are indeed self-coherent and have a distinct meaning, but appear strange because we are unable to reconcile their meaning with our mental life. That is the case when we dream, for instance, that some dear relative has died of plague when we know of no ground for expecting, apprehending, or assuming anything of the sort; we can only ask ourself wonderingly: "What brought that into my head?" To the third group those dreams

belong which are void of both meaning and intelligibility; they are *incoherent, complicated, and meaningless.* The overwhelming number of our dreams partake of this character, and this has given rise to the contemptuous attitude towards dreams and the medical theory of their limited psychical activity. It is especially in the longer and more complicated dream-plots that signs of incoherence are seldom missing.

The contrast between manifest and latent dream-content is clearly only of value for the dreams of the second and more especially for those of the third class. Here are problems which are only solved when the manifest dream is replaced by its latent content; it was an example of this kind, a complicated and unintelligible dream, that we subjected to analysis. Against our expectation we, however, struck upon reasons which prevented a complete cognizance of the latent dream thought. On the repetition of this same experience we were forced to the supposition that there is an *intimate bond, with laws of its own, between the unintelligible and complicated nature of the dream and the difficulties attending communication of the thoughts connected with the dream.* Before investigating the nature of this bond, it will be advantageous to turn our attention to the more readily intelligible dreams of the first class where, the manifest and latent content being identical, the dream work seems to be omitted.

The investigation of these dreams is also advisable from another standpoint. The dreams of *children* are of this nature; they have a meaning, and are not bizarre. This, by the way, is a further objection to reducing dreams to a dissociation of cerebral activity in sleep, for why should such a lowering of psychical functions belong to the nature of sleep in adults, but not in children? We are, however, fully justified in expecting that the explanation of psychical processes in children, essentially simplified as they may be, should serve as an indispensable preparation towards the psychology of the adult.

I shall therefore cite some examples of dreams which I have gathered from children. A girl of nineteen months was made to go without food for a day because she had been sick in the morning, and, according to nurse, had made herself ill through eating strawberries.

During the night, after her day of fasting, she was heard calling out her name during sleep, and adding: "*Tawberry, eggs, pap.*" She is dreaming that she is eating, and selects out of her menu exactly what she supposes she will not get much of just now.

The same kind of dream about a forbidden dish was that of a little boy of twenty-two months. The day before he was told to offer his uncle a present of a small basket of cherries, of which the child was, of course, only allowed one to taste. He woke up with the joyful news: "Hermann eaten up all the cherries."

A girl of three and a half years had made during the day a sea trip which was too short for her, and she cried when she had to get out of the boat. The next morning her story was that during the night she had been on the sea, thus continuing the interrupted trip.

A boy of five and a half years was not at all pleased with his party during a walk in the Dachstein region. Whenever a new peak came into sight he asked if that were the Dachstein, and, finally, refused to accompany the party to the waterfall. His behavior was ascribed to fatigue; but a better explanation was forthcoming when the next morning he told his dream: *he had ascended the Dachstein.* Obviously he expected the ascent of the Dachstein to be the object of the excursion, and was vexed by not getting a glimpse of the mountain. The dream gave him what the day had withheld. The dream of a girl of six was similar; her father had cut short the walk before reaching the promised objective on account of the lateness of the hour. On the way back she noticed a signpost giving the name of another place for excursions; her father promised to take her there also some other day. She greeted her father next day with the news that she had dreamt that *her father had been with her to both places.*

What is common in all these dreams is obvious. They completely satisfy wishes excited during the day which remain unrealized. They are simply and undisguisedly realizations of wishes.

The following child-dream, not quite understandable at first sight, is nothing else than a wish realized. On account of poliomyelitis a girl, not quite four years of age, was brought from the country into

town, and remained over night with a childless aunt in a big–for her, naturally, huge–bed. The next morning she stated that she had dreamt that *the bed was much too small for her, so that she could find no place in it.* To explain this dream as a wish is easy when we remember that to be "big" is a frequently expressed wish of all children. The bigness of the bed reminded Miss Little-Would-be-Big only too forcibly of her smallness. This nasty situation became righted in her dream, and she grew so big that the bed now became too small for her.

Even when children's dreams are complicated and polished, their comprehension as a realization of desire is fairly evident. A boy of eight dreamt that he was being driven with Achilles in a war-chariot, guided by Diomedes. The day before he was assiduously reading about great heroes. It is easy to show that he took these heroes as his models, and regretted that he was not living in those days.

From this short collection a further characteristic of the dreams of children is manifest–*their connection with the life of the day.* The desires which are realized in these dreams are left over from the day or, as a rule, the day previous, and the feeling has become intently emphasized and fixed during the day thoughts. Accidental and indifferent matters, or what must appear so to the child, find no acceptance in the contents of the dream.

Innumerable instances of such dreams of the infantile type can be found among adults also, but, as mentioned, these are mostly exactly like the manifest content. Thus, a random selection of persons will generally respond to thirst at night-time with a dream about drinking, thus striving to get rid of the sensation and to let sleep continue. Many persons frequently have these comforting *dreams* before waking, just when they are called. They then dream that they are already up, that they are washing, or already in school, at the office, etc., where they ought to be at a given time. The night before an intended journey one not infrequently dreams that one has already arrived at the destination; before going to a play or to a party the dream not infrequently anticipates, in impatience, as it were, the expected pleasure. At other times the dream expresses the

realization of the desire somewhat indirectly; some connection, some sequel must be known—the first step towards recognizing the desire. Thus, when a husband related to me the dream of his young wife, that her monthly period had begun, I had to bethink myself that the young wife would have expected a pregnancy if the period had been absent. The dream is then a sign of pregnancy. Its meaning is that it shows the wish realized that pregnancy should not occur just yet. Under unusual and extreme circumstances, these dreams of the infantile type become very frequent. The leader of a polar expedition tells us, for instance, that during the wintering amid the ice the crew, with their monotonous diet and slight rations, dreamt regularly, like children, of fine meals, of mountains of tobacco, and of home.

It is not uncommon that out of some long, complicated and intricate dream one specially lucid part stands out containing unmistakably the realization of a desire, but bound up with much unintelligible matter. On more frequently analyzing the seemingly more transparent dreams of adults, it is astonishing to discover that these are rarely as simple as the dreams of children, and that they cover another meaning beyond that of the realization of a wish.

It would certainly be a simple and convenient solution of the riddle if the work of analysis made it at all possible for us to trace the meaningless and intricate dreams of adults back to the infantile type, to the realization of some intensely experienced desire of the day. But there is no warrant for such an expectation. Their dreams are generally full of the most indifferent and bizarre matter, and no trace of the realization of the wish is to be found in their content.

Before leaving these infantile dreams, which are obviously unrealized desires, we must not fail to mention another chief characteristic of dreams, one that has been long noticed, and one which stands out most clearly in this class. I can replace any of these dreams by a phrase expressing a desire. If the sea trip had only lasted longer; if I were only washed and dressed; if I had only been allowed to keep the cherries instead of giving them to my

uncle. But the dream gives something more than the choice, for here the desire is already realized; its realization is real and actual. The dream presentations consist chiefly, if not wholly, of scenes and mainly of visual sense images. Hence a kind of transformation is not entirely absent in this class of dreams, and this may be fairly designated as the dream work. *An idea merely existing in the region of possibility is replaced by a vision of its accomplishment.*

◆◆◆

II

THE DREAM MECHANISM

We are compelled to assume that such transformation of scene has also taken place in intricate dreams, though we do not know whether it has encountered any possible desire. The dream instanced at the commencement, which we analyzed somewhat thoroughly, did give us occasion in two places to suspect something of the kind. Analysis brought out that my wife was occupied with others at table, and that I did not like it; in the dream itself *exactly the opposite* occurs, for the person who replaces my wife gives me her undivided attention. But can one wish for anything pleasanter after a disagreeable incident than that the exact contrary should have occurred, just as the dream has it? The stinging thought in the analysis, that I have never had anything for nothing, is similarly connected with the woman's remark in the dream: "You have always had such beautiful eyes." Some portion of the opposition between the latent and manifest content of the dream must be therefore derived from the realization of a wish.

Another manifestation of the dream work which all incoherent dreams have in common is still more noticeable. Choose any instance, and compare the number of separate elements in it, or the extent of the dream, if written down, with the dream thoughts yielded by analysis, and of which but a trace can be refound in the dream itself. There can be no doubt that the dream working has resulted in an extraordinary compression or *condensation*. It is not at first easy to form an opinion as to the extent of the condensation; the more

deeply you go into the analysis, the more deeply you are impressed by it. There will be found no factor in the dream whence the chains of associations do not lead in two or more directions, no scene which has not been pieced together out of two or more impressions and events. For instance, I once dreamt about a kind of swimming-bath where the bathers suddenly separated in all directions; at one place on the edge a person stood bending towards one of the bathers as if to drag him out. The scene was a composite one, made up out of an event that occurred at the time of puberty, and of two pictures, one of which I had seen just shortly before the dream. The two pictures were The Surprise in the Bath, from Schwind's Cycle of the Melusine (note the bathers suddenly separating), and The Flood, by an Italian master. The little incident was that I once witnessed a lady, who had tarried in the swimming-bath until the men's hour, being helped out of the water by the swimming-master. The scene in the dream which was selected for analysis led to a whole group of reminiscences, each one of which had contributed to the dream content. First of all came the little episode from the time of my courting, of which I have already spoken; the pressure of a hand under the table gave rise in the dream to the "under the table," which I had subsequently to find a place for in my recollection. There was, of course, at the time not a word about "undivided attention." Analysis taught me that this factor is the realization of a desire through its contradictory and related to the behavior of my wife at the table d'hôte. An exactly similar and much more important episode of our courtship, one which separated us for an entire day, lies hidden behind this recent recollection. The intimacy, the hand resting upon the knee, refers to a quite different connection and to quite other persons. This element in the dream becomes again the starting-point of two distinct series of reminiscences, and so on.

The stuff of the dream thoughts which has been accumulated for the formation of the dream scene must be naturally fit for this application. There must be one or more common factors. The dream work proceeds like Francis Galton with his family photographs. The

different elements are put one on top of the other; what is common to the composite picture stands out clearly, the opposing details cancel each other. This process of reproduction partly explains the wavering statements, of a peculiar vagueness, in so many elements of the dream. For the interpretation of dreams this rule holds good: When analysis discloses *uncertainty*, as to *either—or* read *and*, *taking* each section of the apparent alternatives as a separate outlet for a series of impressions.

When there is nothing in common between the dream thoughts, the dream work takes the trouble to create a something, in order to make a common presentation feasible in the dream. The simplest way to approximate two dream thoughts, which have as yet nothing in common, consists in making such a change in the actual expression of one idea as will meet a slight responsive recasting in the form of the other idea. The process is analogous to that of rhyme, when consonance supplies the desired common factor. A good deal of the dream work consists in the creation of those frequently very witty, but often exaggerated, digressions. These vary from the common presentation in the dream content to dream thoughts which are as varied as are the causes in form and essence which give rise to them. In the analysis of our example of a dream, I find a like case of the transformation of a thought in order that it might agree with another essentially foreign one. In following out the analysis I struck upon the thought: *I should like to have something for nothing.* But this formula is not serviceable to the dream. Hence it is replaced by another one: "I should like to enjoy something free of cost."[1] The word "kost" (taste), with its double meaning, is appropriate to a table d'hôte; it, moreover, is in place through the special sense in the dream. At home if there is a dish which the children decline,

1. "Ich möchte gerne etwas geniessen ohne 'Kosten' zu haben." A a pun upon the word "kosten," which has two meanings—"taste" and "cost." In "Die Traumdeutung," third edition, p. 71 footnote, Professor Freud remarks that "the finest example of dream interpretation left us by the ancients is based upon a pun" (from "The Interpretation of Dreams," by Artemidorus Daldianus). "Moreover, dreams are so intimately bound up with language that Ferenczi truly points out that every tongue has its own language of dreams. A dream is as a rule untranslatable into other languages."—TRANSLATOR.

their mother first tries gentle persuasion, with a "Just taste it." That the dream work should unhesitatingly use the double meaning of the word is certainly remarkable; ample experience has shown, however, that the occurrence is quite usual.

Through condensation of the dream certain constituent parts of its content are explicable which are peculiar to the dream life alone, and which are not found in the waking state. Such are the composite and mixed persons, the extraordinary mixed figures, creations comparable with the fantastic animal compositions of Orientals; a moment's thought and these are reduced to unity, whilst the fancies of the dream are ever formed anew in an inexhaustible profusion. Every one knows such images in his own dreams; manifold are their origins. I can build up a person by borrowing one feature from one person and one from another, or by giving to the form of one the name of another in my dream. I can also visualize one person, but place him in a position which has occurred to another. There is a meaning in all these cases when different persons are amalgamated into one substitute. Such cases denote an "and," a "just like," a comparison of the original person from a certain point of view, a comparison which can be also realized in the dream itself. As a rule, however, the identity of the blended persons is only discoverable by analysis, and is only indicated in the dream content by the formation of the "combined" person.

The same diversity in their ways of formation and the same rules for its solution hold good also for the innumerable medley of dream contents, examples of which I need scarcely adduce. Their strangeness quite disappears when we resolve not to place them on a level with the objects of perception as known to us when awake, but to remember that they represent the art of dream condensation by an exclusion of unnecessary detail. Prominence is given to the common character of the combination. Analysis must also generally supply the common features. The dream says simply: *All these things have an "x" in common.* The decomposition of these mixed images by analysis is often the quickest way to an interpretation of the dream. Thus I once dreamt that I was sitting with one of my former university tutors on a bench, which was undergoing a rapid continuous movement amidst other benches. This

was a combination of lecture-room and moving staircase. I will not pursue the further result of the thought. Another time I was sitting in a carriage, and on my lap an object in shape like a top-hat, which, however, was made of transparent glass. The scene at once brought to my mind the proverb: "He who keeps his hat in his hand will travel safely through the land." By a slight turn the *glass hat* reminded me of *Auer's light*, and I knew that I was about to invent something which was to make me as rich and independent as his invention had made my countryman, Dr. Auer, of Welsbach; then I should be able to travel instead of remaining in Vienna. In the dream I was traveling with my invention, with the, it is true, rather awkward glass top-hat. The dream work is peculiarly adept at representing two contradictory conceptions by means of the same mixed image. Thus, for instance, a woman dreamt of herself carrying a tall flower-stalk, as in the picture of the Annunciation (Chastity-Mary is her own name), but the stalk was bedecked with thick white blossoms resembling camellias (contrast with chastity: La dame aux Camelias).

A great deal of what we have called "dream condensation" can be thus formulated. Each one of the elements of the dream content is *overdetermined* by the matter of the dream thoughts; it is not derived from one element of these thoughts, but from a whole series. These are not necessarily interconnected in any way, but may belong to the most diverse spheres of thought. The dream element truly represents all this disparate matter in the dream content. Analysis, moreover, discloses another side of the relationship between dream content and dream thoughts. Just as one element of the dream leads to associations with several dream thoughts, so, as a rule, the *one dream thought represents more than one dream element.* The threads of the association do not simply converge from the dream thoughts to the dream content, but on the way they overlap and interweave in every way.

Next to the transformation of one thought in the scene (its "dramatization"), condensation is the most important and most characteristic feature of the dream work. We have as yet no clue as to the motive calling for such compression of the content.

In the complicated and intricate dreams with which we are now concerned, condensation and dramatization do not wholly account for the difference between dream contents and dream thoughts. There is evidence of a third factor, which deserves careful consideration.

When I have arrived at an understanding of the dream thoughts by my analysis I notice, above all, that the matter of the manifest is very different from that of the latent dream content. That is, I admit, only an apparent difference which vanishes on closer investigation, for in the end I find the whole dream content carried out in the dream thoughts, nearly all the dream thoughts again represented in the dream content. Nevertheless, there does remain a certain amount of difference.

The essential content which stood out clearly and broadly in the dream must, after analysis, rest satisfied with a very subordinate rôle among the dream thoughts. These very dream thoughts which, going by my feelings, have a claim to the greatest importance are either not present at all in the dream content, or are represented by some remote allusion in some obscure region of the dream. I can thus describe these phenomena: *During the dream work the psychical intensity of those thoughts and conceptions to which it properly pertains flows to others which, in my judgment, have no claim to such emphasis.* There is no other process which contributes so much to concealment of the dream's meaning and to make the connection between the dream content and dream ideas irrecognizable. During this process, which I will call *the dream displacement*, I notice also the psychical intensity, significance, or emotional nature of the thoughts become transposed in sensory vividness. What was clearest in the dream seems to me, without further consideration, the most important; but often in some obscure element of the dream I can recognize the most direct offspring of the principal dream thought.

I could only designate this dream displacement as the *transvaluation of psychical values.* The phenomena will not have been considered in all its bearings unless I add that this displacement or transvaluation is shared by different dreams in extremely varying degrees. There are

dreams which take place almost without any displacement. These have the same time, meaning, and intelligibility as we found in the dreams which recorded a desire. In other dreams not a bit of the dream idea has retained its own psychical value, or everything essential in these dream ideas has been replaced by unessentials, whilst every kind of transition between these conditions can be found. The more obscure and intricate a dream is, the greater is the part to be ascribed to the impetus of displacement in its formation.

The example that we chose for analysis shows, at least, this much of displacement—that its content has a different center of interest from that of the dream ideas. In the forefront of the dream content the main scene appears as if a woman wished to make advances to me; in the dream idea the chief interest rests on the desire to enjoy disinterested love which shall "cost nothing"; this idea lies at the back of the talk about the beautiful eyes and the far-fetched allusion to "spinach."

If we abolish the dream displacement, we attain through analysis quite certain conclusions regarding two problems of the dream which are most disputed—as to what provokes a dream at all, and as to the connection of the dream with our waking life. There are dreams which at once expose their links with the events of the day; in others no trace of such a connection can be found. By the aid of analysis it can be shown that every dream, without any exception, is linked up with our impression of the day, or perhaps it would be more correct to say of the day previous to the dream. The impressions which have incited the dream may be so important that we are not surprised at our being occupied with them whilst awake; in this case we are right in saying that the dream carries on the chief interest of our waking life. More usually, however, when the dream contains anything relating to the impressions of the day, it is so trivial, unimportant, and so deserving of oblivion, that we can only recall it with an effort. The dream content appears, then, even when coherent and intelligible, to be concerned with those indifferent trifles of thought undeserving of our waking interest. The depreciation of dreams is largely due to the predominance of the indifferent and the worthless in their content.

Analysis destroys the appearance upon which this derogatory judgment is based. When the dream content discloses nothing but some indifferent impression as instigating the dream, analysis ever indicates some significant event, which has been replaced by something indifferent with which it has entered into abundant associations. Where the dream is concerned with uninteresting and unimportant conceptions, analysis reveals the numerous associative paths which connect the trivial with the momentous in the psychical estimation of the individual. *It is only the action of displacement if what is indifferent obtains recognition in the dream content instead of those impressions which are really the stimulus, or instead of the things of real interest.* In answering the question as to what provokes the dream, as to the connection of the dream, in the daily troubles, we must say, in terms of the insight given us by replacing the manifest latent dream content: *The dream does never trouble itself about things which are not deserving of our concern during the day, and trivialities which do not trouble us during the day have no power to pursue us whilst asleep.*

What provoked the dream in the example which we have analyzed? The really unimportant event, that a friend invited me to a *free ride in his cab.* The table d'hôte scene in the dream contains an allusion to this indifferent motive, for in conversation I had brought the taxi parallel with the table d'hôte. But I can indicate the important event which has as its substitute the trivial one. A few days before I had disbursed a large sum of money for a member of my family who is very dear to me. Small wonder, says the dream thought, if this person is grateful to me for this–this love is not cost-free. But love that shall cost nothing is one of the prime thoughts of the dream. The fact that shortly before this I had had several *drives* with the relative in question puts the one drive with my friend in a position to recall the connection with the other person. The indifferent impression which, by such ramifications, provokes the dream is subservient to another condition which is not true of the real source of the dream–the impression must be a recent one, everything arising from the day of the dream.

I cannot leave the question of dream displacement without the consideration of a remarkable process in the formation of dreams in which condensation and displacement work together towards one

end. In condensation we have already considered the case where two conceptions in the dream having something in common, some point of contact, are replaced in the dream content by a mixed image, where the distinct germ corresponds to what is common, and the indistinct secondary modifications to what is distinctive. If displacement is added to condensation, there is no formation of a mixed image, but a *common mean* which bears the same relationship to the individual elements as does the resultant in the parallelogram of forces to its components. In one of my dreams, for instance, there is talk of an injection with *propyl*. On first analysis I discovered an indifferent but true incident where *amyl* played a part as the excitant of the dream. I cannot yet vindicate the exchange of amyl for propyl. To the round of ideas of the same dream, however, there belongs the recollection of my first visit to Munich, when the *Propylæa* struck me. The attendant circumstances of the analysis render it admissible that the influence of this second group of conceptions caused the displacement of amyl to propyl. *Propyl* is, so to say, the mean idea between *amyl* and *propylæa*; it got into the dream as a kind of *compromise* by simultaneous condensation and displacement.

The need of discovering some motive for this bewildering work of the dream is even more called for in the case of displacement than in condensation.

Although the work of displacement must be held mainly responsible if the dream thoughts are not refound or recognized in the dream content (unless the motive of the changes be guessed), it is another and milder kind of transformation which will be considered with the dream thoughts which leads to the discovery of a new but readily understood act of the dream work. The first dream thoughts which are unravelled by analysis frequently strike one by their unusual wording. They do not appear to be expressed in the sober form which our thinking prefers; rather are they expressed symbolically by allegories and metaphors like the figurative language of the poets. It is not difficult to find the motives for this degree of constraint in the expression of dream ideas. The dream content consists chiefly

of visual scenes; hence the dream ideas must, in the first place, be prepared to make use of these forms of presentation. Conceive that a political leader's or a barrister's address had to be transposed into pantomime, and it will be easy to understand the transformations to which the dream work is constrained by regard for this *dramatization of the dream content.*

Around the psychical stuff of dream thoughts there are ever found reminiscences of impressions, not infrequently of early childhood—scenes which, as a rule, have been visually grasped. Whenever possible, this portion of the dream ideas exercises a definite influence upon the modelling of the dream content; it works like a center of crystallization, by attracting and rearranging the stuff of the dream thoughts. The scene of the dream is not infrequently nothing but a modified repetition, complicated by interpolations of events that have left such an impression; the dream but very seldom reproduces accurate and unmixed reproductions of real scenes.

The dream content does not, however, consist exclusively of scenes, but it also includes scattered fragments of visual images, conversations, and even bits of unchanged thoughts. It will be perhaps to the point if we instance in the briefest way the means of dramatization which are at the disposal of the dream work for the repetition of the dream thoughts in the peculiar language of the dream.

The dream thoughts which we learn from the analysis exhibit themselves as a psychical complex of the most complicated superstructure. Their parts stand in the most diverse relationship to each other; they form backgrounds and foregrounds, stipulations, digressions, illustrations, demonstrations, and protestations. It may be said to be almost the rule that one train of thought is followed by its contradictory. No feature known to our reason whilst awake is absent. If a dream is to grow out of all this, the psychical matter is submitted to a pressure which condenses it extremely, to an inner shrinking and displacement, creating at the same time fresh surfaces, to a selective interweaving among the constituents best adapted for the construction of these scenes. Having regard to the origin of this stuff,

the term *regression* can be fairly applied to this process. The logical chains which hitherto held the psychical stuff together become lost in this transformation to the dream content. The dream work takes on, as it were, only the essential content of the dream thoughts for elaboration. It is left to analysis to restore the connection which the dream work has destroyed.

The dream's means of expression must therefore be regarded as meager in comparison with those of our imagination, though the dream does not renounce all claims to the restitution of logical relation to the dream thoughts. It rather succeeds with tolerable frequency in replacing these by formal characters of its own.

By reason of the undoubted connection existing between all the parts of dream thoughts, the dream is able to embody this matter into a single scene. It upholds a *logical connection* as *approximation in time and space*, just as the painter, who groups all the poets for his picture of Parnassus who, though they have never been all together on a mountain peak, yet form ideally a community. The dream continues this method of presentation in individual dreams, and often when it displays two elements close together in the dream content it warrants some special inner connection between what they represent in the dream thoughts. It should be, moreover, observed that all the dreams of one night prove on analysis to originate from the same sphere of thought.

The causal connection between two ideas is either left without presentation, or replaced by two different long portions of dreams one after the other. This presentation is frequently a reversed one, the beginning of the dream being the deduction, and its end the hypothesis. The direct *transformation* of one thing into another in the dream seems to serve the relationship of *cause* and *effect.*

The dream never utters the *alternative "either-or,"* but accepts both as having equal rights in the same connection. When "either-or" is used in the reproduction of dreams, it is, as I have already mentioned, to be replaced by "*and*."

Conceptions which stand in opposition to one another are preferably expressed in dreams by the same element.[2] There seems no "not" in dreams. Opposition between two ideas, the relation of conversion, is represented in dreams in a very remarkable way. It is expressed by the reversal of another part of the dream content just as if by way of appendix. We shall later on deal with another form of expressing disagreement. The common dream sensation of *movement checked* serves the purpose of representing disagreement of impulses—a *conflict of the will.*

Only one of the logical relationships—that of *similarity, identity, agreement*—is found highly developed in the mechanism of dream formation. Dream work makes use of these cases as a starting-point for condensation, drawing together everything which shows such agreement to a *fresh unity.*

These short, crude observations naturally do not suffice as an estimate of the abundance of the dream's formal means of presenting the logical relationships of the dream thoughts. In this respect, individual dreams are worked up more nicely or more carelessly, our text will have been followed more or less closely, auxiliaries of the dream work will have been taken more or less into consideration. In the latter case they appear obscure, intricate, incoherent. When the dream appears openly absurd, when it contains an obvious paradox in its content, it is so of purpose. Through its apparent disregard of all logical claims, it expresses a part of the intellectual content of the

---

2. It is worthy of remark that eminent philologists maintain that the oldest languages used the same word for expressing quite general antitheses. In C. Abel's essay, "Ueber den Gegensinn der Urworter" (1884, the following examples of such words in England are given: "gleam—gloom"; "to lock—loch"; "down—The Downs"; "to step—to stop." In his essay on "The Origin of Language" ("Linguistic Essays," p. 240), Abel says: "When the Englishman says 'without,' is not his judgment based upon the comparative juxtaposition of two opposites, 'with' and 'out'; 'with' itself originally meant 'without,' as may still be seen in 'withdraw.' 'Bid' includes the opposite sense of giving and of proffering." Abel, "The English Verbs of Command," "Linguistic Essays," p. 104; see also Freud, "Ueber den Gegensinn der Urworte"; *Jahrbuch für Psychoanalytische und Psychopathologische Forschungen*, Band II., part i., p. 179).—TRANSLATOR.

dream ideas. Absurdity in the dream denotes *disagreement, scorn, disdain* in the dream thoughts. As this explanation is in entire disagreement with the view that the dream owes its origin to dissociated, uncritical cerebral activity, I will emphasize my view by an example:

"One of my acquaintances, Mr. M____, has been attacked by no less a person than Goethe in an essay with, we all maintain, unwarrantable violence. Mr. M____ has naturally been ruined by this attack. He complains very bitterly of this at a dinner-party, but his respect for Goethe has not diminished through this personal experience. I now attempt to clear up the chronological relations which strike me as improbable. Goethe died in 1832. As his attack upon Mr. M____ must, of course, have taken place before, Mr. M____ must have been then a very young man. It seems to me plausible that he was eighteen. I am not certain, however, what year we are actually in, and the whole calculation falls into obscurity. The attack was, moreover, contained in Goethe's well-known essay on 'Nature.'"

The absurdity of the dream becomes the more glaring when I state that Mr. M____ is a young business man without any poetical or literary interests. My analysis of the dream will show what method there is in this madness. The dream has derived its material from three sources:

Mr. M____, to whom I was introduced at a dinner-party, begged me one day to examine his elder brother, who showed signs of mental trouble. In conversation with the patient, an unpleasant episode occurred. Without the slightest occasion he disclosed one of his brother's *youthful escapades*. I had asked the patient the *year of his birth* (*year of death* in dream), and led him to various calculations which might show up his want of memory.

A medical journal which displayed my name among others on the cover had published a *ruinous* review of a book by my friend F____ of Berlin, from the pen of a very *juvenile* reviewer. I communicated with the editor, who, indeed, expressed his regret, but would not promise any redress. Thereupon I broke off my connection with the paper; in

my letter of resignation I expressed the hope that our *personal relations would not suffer from this.* Here is the real source of the dream. The derogatory reception of my friend's work had made a deep impression upon me. In my judgment, it contained a fundamental biological discovery which only now, several years later, commences to find favor among the professors.

A little while before, a patient gave me the medical history of her brother, who, exclaiming "*Nature, Nature!*" had gone out of his mind. The doctors considered that the exclamation arose from a study of *Goethe's* beautiful essay, and indicated that the patient had been overworking. I expressed the opinion that it seemed more *plausible* to me that the exclamation "Nature!" was to be taken in that sexual meaning known also to the less educated in our country. It seemed to me that this view had something in it, because the unfortunate youth afterwards mutilated his genital organs. The patient was eighteen years old when the attack occurred.

The first person in the dream-thoughts behind the ego was my friend who had been so scandalously treated. "*I now attempted to clear up the chronological relation.*" My friend's book deals with the chronological relations of life, and, amongst other things, correlates *Goethe's* duration of life with a number of days in many ways important to biology. The ego is, however, represented as a general paralytic ("*I am not certain what year we are actually in*"). The dream exhibits my friend as behaving like a general paralytic, and thus riots in absurdity. But the dream thoughts run ironically. "Of course he is a madman, a fool, and you are the genius who understands all about it. But shouldn't it be the *other way round?*" This inversion obviously took place in the dream when Goethe attacked the young man, which is absurd, whilst any one, however young, can to-day easily attack the great Goethe.

I am prepared to maintain that no dream is inspired by other than egoistic emotions. The ego in the dream does not, indeed, represent only my friend, but stands for myself also. I identify myself with him because the fate of his discovery appears to me typical of the acceptance of *my own.* If I were to publish my own theory, which gives

sexuality predominance in the ætiology of psychoneurotic disorders (see the allusion to the eighteen-year-old patient–"*Nature, Nature!*"), the same criticism would be leveled at me, and it would even now meet with the same contempt.

When I follow out the dream thoughts closely, I ever find only *scorn* and *contempt* as *correlated with the dream's absurdity*. It is well known that the discovery of a cracked sheep's skull on the Lido in Venice gave Goethe the hint for the so-called vertebral theory of the skull. My friend plumes himself on having as a student raised a hubbub for the resignation of an aged professor who had done good work (including some in this very subject of comparative anatomy), but who, on account of *decrepitude*, had become quite incapable of teaching. The agitation my friend inspired was so successful because in the German Universities an *age limit* is not demanded for academic work. *Age is no protection against folly.* In the hospital here I had for years the honor to serve under a chief who, long fossilized, was for decades notoriously *feebleminded*, and was yet permitted to continue in his responsible office. A trait, after the manner of the find in the Lido, forces itself upon me here. It was to this man that some youthful colleagues in the hospital adapted the then popular slang of that day: "No Goethe has written that," "No Schiller composed that," etc.

We have not exhausted our valuation of the dream work. In addition to condensation, displacement, and definite arrangement of the psychical matter, we must ascribe to it yet another activity–one which is, indeed, not shared by every dream. I shall not treat this position of the dream work exhaustively; I will only point out that the readiest way to arrive at a conception of it is to take for granted, probably unfairly, that it *only subsequently influences the dream content which has already been built up*. Its mode of action thus consists in so coördinating the parts of the dream that these coalesce to a coherent whole, to a dream composition. The dream gets a kind of façade which, it is true, does not conceal the whole of its content. There is a sort of preliminary explanation to be strengthened by

interpolations and slight alterations. Such elaboration of the dream content must not be too pronounced; the misconception of the dream thoughts to which it gives rise is merely superficial, and our first piece of work in analyzing a dream is to get rid of these early attempts at interpretation.

The motives for this part of the dream work are easily gauged. This final elaboration of the dream is due to a *regard for intelligibility*—a fact at once betraying the origin of an action which behaves towards the actual dream content just as our normal psychical action behaves towards some proffered perception that is to our liking. The dream content is thus secured under the pretense of certain expectations, is perceptually classified by the supposition of its intelligibility, thereby risking its falsification, whilst, in fact, the most extraordinary misconceptions arise if the dream can be correlated with nothing familiar. Every one is aware that we are unable to look at any series of unfamiliar signs, or to listen to a discussion of unknown words, without at once making perpetual changes through *our regard for intelligibility*, through our falling back upon what is familiar.

We can call those dreams *properly made up* which are the result of an elaboration in every way analogous to the psychical action of our waking life. In other dreams there is no such action; not even an attempt is made to bring about order and meaning. We regard the dream as "quite mad," because on awaking it is with this last-named part of the dream work, the dream elaboration, that we identify ourselves. So far, however, as our analysis is concerned, the dream, which resembles a medley of disconnected fragments, is of as much value as the one with a smooth and beautifully polished surface. In the former case we are spared, to some extent, the trouble of breaking down the super-elaboration of the dream content.

All the same, it would be an error to see in the dream façade nothing but the misunderstood and somewhat arbitrary elaboration of the dream carried out at the instance of our psychical life. Wishes

and phantasies are not infrequently employed in the erection of this façade, which were already fashioned in the dream thoughts; they are akin to those of our waking life–"day-dreams," as they are very properly called. These wishes and phantasies, which analysis discloses in our dreams at night, often present themselves as repetitions and refashionings of the scenes of infancy. Thus the dream façade may show us directly the true core of the dream, distorted through admixture with other matter.

Beyond these four activities there is nothing else to be discovered in the dream work. If we keep closely to the definition that dream work denotes the transference of dream thoughts to dream content, we are compelled to say that the dream work is not creative; it develops no fancies of its own, it judges nothing, decides nothing. It does nothing but prepare the matter for condensation and displacement, and refashions it for dramatization, to which must be added the inconstant last-named mechanism–that of explanatory elaboration. It is true that a good deal is found in the dream content which might be understood as the result of another and more intellectual performance; but analysis shows conclusively every time that these *intellectual operations were already present in the dream thoughts, and have only been taken over by the dream content.* A syllogism in the dream is nothing other than the repetition of a syllogism in the dream thoughts; it seems inoffensive if it has been transferred to the dream without alteration; it becomes absurd if in the dream work it has been transferred to other matter. A calculation in the dream content simply means that there was a calculation in the dream thoughts; whilst this is always correct, the calculation in the dream can furnish the silliest results by the condensation of its factors and the displacement of the same operations to other things. Even speeches which are found in the dream content are not new compositions; they prove to be pieced together out of speeches which have been made or heard or read; the words are faithfully copied, but the occasion of their utterance is quite overlooked, and their meaning is most violently changed.

It is, perhaps, not superfluous to support these assertions by examples:

1. *A seemingly inoffensive, well-made dream of a patient. She was going to market with her cook, who carried the basket. The butcher said to her when she asked him for something: "That is all gone," and wished to give her something else, remarking; "That's very good." She declines, and goes to the greengrocer, who wants to sell her a peculiar vegetable which is bound up in bundles and of a black color. She says: "I don't know that; I won't take it."*

The remark "That is all gone" arose from the treatment. A few days before I said myself to the patient that the earliest reminiscences of childhood *are all gone* as such, but are replaced by transferences and dreams. Thus I am the butcher.

The second remark, *"I don't know that"* arose in a very different connection. The day before she had herself called out in rebuke to the cook (who, moreover, also appears in the dream): "*Behave yourself properly*; I don't know *that*"—that is, "I don't know this kind of behavior; I won't have it." The more harmless portion of this speech was arrived at by a displacement of the dream content; in the dream thoughts only the other portion of the speech played a part, because the dream work changed an imaginary situation into utter irrecognizability and complete inoffensiveness (while in a certain sense I behave in an unseemly way to the lady). The situation resulting in this phantasy is, however, nothing but a new edition of one that actually took place.

2. A dream apparently meaningless relates to figures. *"She wants to pay something; her daughter takes three florins sixty-five kreuzers out of her purse; but she says: 'What are you doing? It only cost twenty-one kreuzers.'"*

The dreamer was a stranger who had placed her child at school in Vienna, and who was able to continue under my treatment so long as her daughter remained at Vienna. The day before the dream the directress of the school had recommended her to keep the child another year at school. In this case she would have been able to prolong her treatment by one year. The figures in the dream become important if it be remembered that time is money. One year equals 365 days, or, expressed in kreuzers, 365 kreuzers, which is three florins sixty-five kreuzers. The twenty-one kreuzers correspond with the three weeks which remained from the

day of the dream to the end of the school term, and thus to the end of the treatment. It was obviously financial considerations which had moved the lady to refuse the proposal of the directress, and which were answerable for the triviality of the amount in the dream.

3. *A lady, young, but already ten years married, heard that a friend of hers, Miss Elise L____, of about the same age, had become engaged. This gave rise to the following dream:*

She was sitting with her husband in the theater; the one side of the stalls was quite empty. Her husband tells her, Elise L____ and her fiancé had intended coming, but could only get some cheap seats, three for one florin fifty kreuzers, and these they would not take. In her opinion, that would not have mattered very much.

The origin of the figures from the matter of the dream thoughts and the changes the figures underwent are of interest. Whence came the one florin fifty kreuzers? From a trifling occurrence of the previous day. Her sister-in-law had received 150 florins as a present from her husband, and had quickly got rid of it by buying some ornament. Note that 150 florins is one hundred times one florin fifty kreuzers. For the *three* concerned with the tickets, the only link is that Elise L____ is exactly three months younger than the dreamer. The scene in the dream is the repetition of a little adventure for which she has often been teased by her husband. She was once in a great hurry to get tickets in time for a piece, and when she came to the theater *one side of the stalls was almost empty*. It was therefore quite unnecessary for her to have been in *such a hurry*. Nor must we overlook the absurdity of the dream that two persons should take three tickets for the theater.

Now for the dream ideas. It was *stupid* to have married so early; I *need not* have been *in so great a hurry*. Elise L____'s example shows me that I should have been able to get a husband later; indeed, one a *hundred times better* if I had but waited. I could have bought *three* such men with the money (dowry).

◆◆◆

III

WHY THE DREAM DISGUISES THE DESIRES

In the foregoing exposition we have now learnt something of the dream work; we must regard it as a quite special psychical process, which, so far as we are aware, resembles nothing else. To the dream work has been transferred that bewilderment which its product, the dream, has aroused in us. In truth, the dream work is only the first recognition of a group of psychical processes to which must be referred the origin of hysterical symptoms, the ideas of morbid dread, obsession, and illusion. Condensation, and especially displacement, are never-failing features in these other processes. The regard for appearance remains, on the other hand, peculiar to the dream work. If this explanation brings the dream into line with the formation of psychical disease, it becomes the more important to fathom the essential conditions of processes like dream building. It will be probably a surprise to hear that neither the state of sleep nor illness is among the indispensable conditions. A whole number of phenomena of the everyday life of healthy persons, forgetfulness, slips in speaking and in holding things, together with a certain class of mistakes, are due to a psychical mechanism analogous to that of the dream and the other members of this group.

Displacement is the core of the problem, and the most striking of all the dream performances. A thorough investigation of the subject shows that the essential condition of displacement is purely psychological; it is in the nature of a motive. We get on the track by thrashing out experiences which one cannot avoid in the analysis

of dreams. I had to break off the relations of my dream thoughts in the analysis of my dream on p. 8 because I found some experiences which I do not wish strangers to know, and which I could not relate without serious damage to important considerations. I added, it would be no use were I to select another instead of that particular dream; in every dream where the content is obscure or intricate, I should hit upon dream thoughts which call for secrecy. If, however, I continue the analysis for myself, without regard to those others, for whom, indeed, so personal an event as my dream cannot matter, I arrive finally at ideas which surprise me, which I have not known to be mine, which not only appear *foreign* to me, but which are *unpleasant*, and which I would like to oppose vehemently, whilst the chain of ideas running through the analysis intrudes upon me inexorably. I can only take these circumstances into account by admitting that these thoughts are actually part of my psychical life, possessing a certain psychical intensity or energy. However, by virtue of a particular psychological condition, the *thoughts could not become conscious to me.* I call this particular condition "*Repression.*" It is therefore impossible for me not to recognize some casual relationship between the obscurity of the dream content and this state of repression—this *incapacity of consciousness.* Whence I conclude that the cause of the obscurity is *the desire to conceal these thoughts.* Thus I arrive at the conception of the *dream distortion* as the deed of the dream work, and of *displacement* serving to disguise this object.

I will test this in my own dream, and ask myself, What is the thought which, quite innocuous in its distorted form, provokes my liveliest opposition in its real form? I remember that the free drive reminded me of the last expensive drive with a member of my family, the interpretation of the dream being: I should for once like to experience affection for which I should not have to pay, and that shortly before the dream I had to make a heavy disbursement for this very person. In this connection, I cannot get away from the thought *that I regret this disbursement.* It is only when I acknowledge this feeling that there is any sense in my wishing in the dream for an affection that should entail no outlay. And yet I can state on

my honor that I did not hesitate for a moment when it became necessary to expend that sum. The regret, the counter-current, was unconscious to me. Why it was unconscious is quite another question which would lead us far away from the answer which, though within my knowledge, belongs elsewhere.

If I subject the dream of another person instead of one of my own to analysis, the result is the same; the motives for convincing others is, however, changed. In the dream of a healthy person the only way for me to enable him to accept this repressed idea is the coherence of the dream thoughts. He is at liberty to reject this explanation. But if we are dealing with a person suffering from any neurosis—say from hysteria—the recognition of these repressed ideas is compulsory by reason of their connection with the symptoms of his illness and of the improvement resulting from exchanging the symptoms for the repressed ideas. Take the patient from whom I got the last dream about the three tickets for one florin fifty kreuzers. Analysis shows that she does not think highly of her husband, that she regrets having married him, that she would be glad to change him for some one else. It is true that she maintains that she loves her husband, that her emotional life knows nothing about this depreciation (a hundred times better!), but all her symptoms lead to the same conclusion as this dream. When her repressed memories had rewakened a certain period when she was conscious that she did not love her husband, her symptoms disappeared, and therewith disappeared her resistance to the interpretation of the dream.

This conception of repression once fixed, together with the distortion of the dream in relation to repressed psychical matter, we are in a position to give a general exposition of the principal results which the analysis of dreams supplies. We learnt that the most intelligible and meaningful dreams are unrealized desires; the desires they pictured as realized are known to consciousness, have been held over from the daytime, and are of absorbing interest. The analysis of obscure and intricate dreams discloses something very similar; the dream scene again pictures as realized some desire which regularly

proceeds from the dream ideas, but the picture is unrecognizable, and is only cleared up in the analysis. The desire itself is either one repressed, foreign to consciousness, or it is closely bound up with repressed ideas. The formula for these dreams may be thus stated: *They are concealed realizations of repressed desires.* It is interesting to note that they are right who regard the dream as foretelling the future. Although the future which the dream shows us is not that which will occur, but that which we would like to occur. Folk psychology proceeds here according to its wont; it believes what it wishes to believe.

Dreams can be divided into three classes according to their relation towards the realization of desire. Firstly come those which exhibit a *non-repressed, non-concealed desire*; these are dreams of the infantile type, becoming ever rarer among adults. Secondly, dreams which express in *veiled* form some *repressed desire*; these constitute by far the larger number of our dreams, and they require analysis for their understanding. Thirdly, these dreams where repression exists, but *without* or with but slight concealment. These dreams are invariably accompanied by a feeling of dread which brings the dream to an end. This feeling of dread here replaces dream displacement; I regarded the dream work as having prevented this in the dream of the second class. It is not very difficult to prove that what is now present as intense dread in the dream was once desire, and is now secondary to the repression.

There are also definite dreams with a painful content, without the presence of any anxiety in the dream. These cannot be reckoned among dreams of dread; they have, however, always been used to prove the unimportance and the psychical futility of dreams. An analysis of such an example will show that it belongs to our second class of dreams—a *perfectly concealed* realization of repressed desires. Analysis will demonstrate at the same time how excellently adapted is the work of displacement to the concealment of desires.

A girl dreamt that she saw lying dead before her the only surviving child of her sister amid the same surroundings as a few years before she saw the first child lying dead. She was not sensible of any pain, but naturally combatted the view that the scene represented a desire of hers.

Nor was that view necessary. Years ago it was at the funeral of the child that she had last seen and spoken to the man she loved. Were the second child to die, she would be sure to meet this man again in her sister's house. She is longing to meet him, but struggles against this feeling. The day of the dream she had taken a ticket for a lecture, which announced the presence of the man she always loved. The dream is simply a dream of impatience common to those which happen before a journey, theater, or simply anticipated pleasures. The longing is concealed by the shifting of the scene to the occasion when any joyous feeling were out of place, and yet where it did once exist. Note, further, that the emotional behavior in the dream is adapted, not to the displaced, but to the real but suppressed dream ideas. The scene anticipates the long-hoped-for meeting; there is here no call for painful emotions.

There has hitherto been no occasion for philosophers to bestir themselves with a psychology of repression. We must be allowed to construct some clear conception as to the origin of dreams as the first steps in this unknown territory. The scheme which we have formulated not only from a study of dreams is, it is true, already somewhat complicated, but we cannot find any simpler one that will suffice. We hold that our psychical apparatus contains two procedures for the construction of thoughts. The second one has the advantage that its products find an open path to consciousness, whilst the activity of the first procedure is unknown to itself, and can only arrive at consciousness through the second one. At the borderland of these two procedures, where the first passes over into the second, a censorship is established which only passes what pleases it, keeping back everything else. That which is rejected by the censorship is, according to our definition, in a state of repression. Under certain conditions, one of which is the sleeping state, the balance of power between the two procedures is so changed that what is repressed can no longer be kept back. In the sleeping state this may possibly occur through the negligence of the censor; what has been hitherto repressed will now succeed in finding its way to consciousness. But as the censorship is never absent, but merely off guard, certain alterations must be conceded so as to placate it. It is a compromise

which becomes conscious in this case—a compromise between what one procedure has in view and the demands of the other. *Repression, laxity of the censor, compromise*—this is the foundation for the origin of many another psychological process, just as it is for the dream. In such compromises we can observe the processes of condensation, of displacement, the acceptance of superficial associations, which we have found in the dream work.

It is not for us to deny the demonic element which has played a part in constructing our explanation of dream work. The impression left is that the formation of obscure dreams proceeds as if a person had something to say which must be agreeable for another person upon whom he is dependent to hear. It is by the use of this image that we figure to ourselves the conception of the *dream distortion* and of the censorship, and ventured to crystallize our impression in a rather crude, but at least definite, psychological theory. Whatever explanation the future may offer of these first and second procedures, we shall expect a confirmation of our correlate that the second procedure commands the entrance to consciousness, and can exclude the first from consciousness.

Once the sleeping state overcome, the censorship resumes complete sway, and is now able to revoke that which was granted in a moment of weakness. That the *forgetting* of dreams explains this in part, at least, we are convinced by our experience, confirmed again and again. During the relation of a dream, or during analysis of one, it not infrequently happens that some fragment of the dream is suddenly forgotten. This fragment so forgotten invariably contains the best and readiest approach to an understanding of the dream. Probably that is why it sinks into oblivion—*i.e.*, into a renewed suppression.

Viewing the dream content as the representation of a realized desire, and referring its vagueness to the changes made by the censor in the repressed matter, it is no longer difficult to grasp the function of dreams. In fundamental contrast with those saws which assume that sleep is disturbed by dreams, we hold the *dream as the guardian of sleep*. So far as children's dreams are concerned, our view should find ready acceptance.

The sleeping state or the psychical change to sleep, whatsoever it be, is brought about by the child being sent to sleep or compelled thereto by fatigue, only assisted by the removal of all stimuli which might open other objects to the psychical apparatus. The means which serve to keep external stimuli distant are known; but what are the means we can employ to depress the internal psychical stimuli which frustrate sleep? Look at a mother getting her child to sleep. The child is full of beseeching; he wants another kiss; he wants to play yet awhile. His requirements are in part met, in part drastically put off till the following day. Clearly these desires and needs, which agitate him, are hindrances to sleep. Every one knows the charming story of the bad boy (Baldwin Groller's) who awoke at night bellowing out, "*I want the rhinoceros.*" A really good boy, instead of bellowing, would have *dreamt* that he was playing with the rhinoceros. Because the dream which realizes his desire is believed during sleep, it removes the desire and makes sleep possible. It cannot be denied that this belief accords with the dream image, because it is arrayed in the psychical appearance of probability; the child is without the capacity which it will acquire later to distinguish hallucinations or phantasies from reality.

The adult has learnt this differentiation; he has also learnt the futility of desire, and by continuous practice manages to postpone his aspirations, until they can be granted in some roundabout method by a change in the external world. For this reason it is rare for him to have his wishes realized during sleep in the short psychical way. It is even possible that this never happens, and that everything which appears to us like a child's dream demands a much more elaborate explanation. Thus it is that for adults—for every sane person without exception—a differentiation of the psychical matter has been fashioned which the child knew not. A psychical procedure has been reached which, informed by the experience of life, exercises with jealous power a dominating and restraining influence upon psychical emotions; by its relation to consciousness, and by its spontaneous mobility, it is endowed with the greatest means of psychical power. A portion of the infantile emotions has been withheld from this procedure as useless to life, and all the thoughts which flow from these are found in the state of repression.

Whilst the procedure in which we recognize our normal ego reposes upon the desire for sleep, it appears compelled by the psycho-physiological conditions of sleep to abandon some of the energy with which it was wont during the day to keep down what was repressed. This neglect is really harmless; however much the emotions of the child's spirit may be stirred, they find the approach to consciousness rendered difficult, and that to movement blocked in consequence of the state of sleep. The danger of their disturbing sleep must, however, be avoided. Moreover, we must admit that even in deep sleep some amount of free attention is exerted as a protection against sense-stimuli which might, perchance, make an awakening seem wiser than the continuance of sleep. Otherwise we could not explain the fact of our being always awakened by stimuli of certain quality. As the old physiologist Burdach pointed out, the mother is awakened by the whimpering of her child, the miller by the cessation of his mill, most people by gently calling out their names. This attention, thus on the alert, makes use of the internal stimuli arising from repressed desires, and fuses them into the dream, which as a compromise satisfies both procedures at the same time. The dream creates a form of psychical release for the wish which is either suppressed or formed by the aid of repression, inasmuch as it presents it as realized. The other procedure is also satisfied, since the continuance of the sleep is assured. Our ego here gladly behaves like a child; it makes the dream pictures believable, saying, as it were, "Quite right, but let me sleep." The contempt which, once awakened, we bear the dream, and which rests upon the absurdity and apparent illogicality of the dream, is probably nothing but the reasoning of our sleeping ego on the feelings about what was repressed; with greater right it should rest upon the incompetency of this disturber of our sleep. In sleep we are now and then aware of this contempt; the dream content transcends the censorship rather too much, we think, "It's only a dream," and sleep on.

It is no objection to this view if there are borderlines for the dream where its function, to preserve sleep from interruption, can no longer be maintained–as in the dreams of impending dread. It is here changed for another function–to suspend the sleep at the proper time. It acts like a conscientious night-watchman, who

first does his duty by quelling disturbances so as not to waken the citizen, but equally does his duty quite properly when he awakens the street should the causes of the trouble seem to him serious and himself unable to cope with them alone.

This function of dreams becomes especially well marked when there arises some incentive for the sense perception. That the senses aroused during sleep influence the dream is well known, and can be experimentally verified; it is one of the certain but much overestimated results of the medical investigation of dreams. Hitherto there has been an insoluble riddle connected with this discovery. The stimulus to the sense by which the investigator affects the sleeper is not properly recognized in the dream, but is intermingled with a number of indefinite interpretations, whose determination appears left to psychical free-will. There is, of course, no such psychical free-will. To an external sense-stimulus the sleeper can react in many ways. Either he awakens or he succeeds in sleeping on. In the latter case he can make use of the dream to dismiss the external stimulus, and this, again, in more ways than one. For instance, he can stay the stimulus by dreaming of a scene which is absolutely intolerable to him. This was the means used by one who was troubled by a painful perineal abscess. He dreamt that he was on horseback, and made use of the poultice, which was intended to alleviate his pain, as a saddle, and thus got away from the cause of the trouble. Or, as is more frequently the case, the external stimulus undergoes a new rendering, which leads him to connect it with a repressed desire seeking its realization, and robs him of its reality, and is treated as if it were a part of the psychical matter. Thus, some one dreamt that he had written a comedy which embodied a definite *motif*; it was being performed; the first act was over amid enthusiastic applause; there was great clapping. At this moment the dreamer must have succeeded in prolonging his sleep despite the disturbance, for when he woke he no longer heard the noise; he concluded rightly that some one must have been beating a carpet or bed. The dreams which come with a loud noise just before waking have all attempted to cover the stimulus to waking by some other explanation, and thus to prolong the sleep for a little while.

Whosoever has firmly accepted this *censorship* as the chief motive for the distortion of dreams will not be surprised to learn as the result of dream interpretation that most of the dreams of adults are traced by analysis to erotic desires. This assertion is not drawn from dreams obviously of a sexual nature, which are known to all dreamers from their own experience, and are the only ones usually described as "sexual dreams." These dreams are ever sufficiently mysterious by reason of the choice of persons who are made the objects of sex, the removal of all the barriers which cry halt to the dreamer's sexual needs in his waking state, the many strange reminders as to details of what are called perversions. But analysis discovers that, in many other dreams in whose manifest content nothing erotic can be found, the work of interpretation shows them up as, in reality, realization of sexual desires; whilst, on the other hand, that much of the thought-making when awake, the thoughts saved us as surplus from the day only, reaches presentation in dreams with the help of repressed erotic desires.

Towards the explanation of this statement, which is no theoretical postulate, it must be remembered that no other class of instincts has required so vast a suppression at the behest of civilization as the sexual, whilst their mastery by the highest psychical processes are in most persons soonest of all relinquished. Since we have learnt to understand *infantile sexuality*, often so vague in its expression, so invariably overlooked and misunderstood, we are justified in saying that nearly every civilized person has retained at some point or other the infantile type of sex life; thus we understand that repressed infantile sex desires furnish the most frequent and most powerful impulses for the formation of dreams.[3]

If the dream, which is the expression of some erotic desire, succeeds in making its manifest content appear innocently asexual, it is only possible in one way. The matter of these sexual presentations cannot be exhibited as such, but must be replaced by allusions, suggestions, and similar indirect means; differing from other cases of indirect presentation,

3. Freud, "Three Contributions to Sexual Theory," translated by A.A. Brill (*Journal of Nervous and Mental Disease Publishing Company, New York*).

those used in dreams must be deprived of direct understanding. The means of presentation which answer these requirements are commonly termed "symbols." A special interest has been directed towards these, since it has been observed that the dreamers of the same language use the like symbols–indeed, that in certain cases community of symbol is greater than community of speech. Since the dreamers do not themselves know the meaning of the symbols they use, it remains a puzzle whence arises their relationship with what they replace and denote. The fact itself is undoubted, and becomes of importance for the technique of the interpretation of dreams, since by the aid of a knowledge of this symbolism it is possible to understand the meaning of the elements of a dream, or parts of a dream, occasionally even the whole dream itself, without having to question the dreamer as to his own ideas. We thus come near to the popular idea of an interpretation of dreams, and, on the other hand, possess again the technique of the ancients, among whom the interpretation of dreams was identical with their explanation through symbolism.

Though the study of dream symbolism is far removed from finality, we now possess a series of general statements and of particular observations which are quite certain. There are symbols which practically always have the same meaning: Emperor and Empress (King and Queen) always mean the parents; room, a woman[4], and so on. The sexes are represented by a great variety of symbols, many of which would be at first quite incomprehensible had not the clews to the meaning been often obtained through other channels.

There are symbols of universal circulation, found in all dreamers, of one range of speech and culture; there are others of the narrowest individual significance which an individual has built up out of his own material. In the first class those can be differentiated whose claim can be at once recognized by the replacement of sexual things

---

4. The words from "and" to "channels" in the next sentence is a short summary of the passage in the original. As this book will be read by other than professional people the passage has not been translated, in deference to English opinion.—TRANSLATOR.

in common speech (those, for instance, arising from agriculture, as reproduction, seed) from others whose sexual references appear to reach back to the earliest times and to the obscurest depths of our image-building. The power of building symbols in both these special forms of symbols has not died out. Recently discovered things, like the airship, are at once brought into universal use as sex symbols.

It would be quite an error to suppose that a profounder knowledge of dream symbolism (the "Language of Dreams") would make us independent of questioning the dreamer regarding his impressions about the dream, and would give us back the whole technique of ancient dream interpreters. Apart from individual symbols and the variations in the use of what is general, one never knows whether an element in the dream is to be understood symbolically or in its proper meaning; the whole content of the dream is certainly not to be interpreted symbolically. The knowledge of dream symbols will only help us in understanding portions of the dream content, and does not render the use of the technical rules previously given at all superfluous. But it must be of the greatest service in interpreting a dream just when the impressions of the dreamer are withheld or are insufficient.

Dream symbolism proves also indispensable for understanding the so-called "typical" dreams and the dreams that "repeat themselves." Dream symbolism leads us far beyond the dream; it does not belong only to dreams, but is likewise dominant in legend, myth, and saga, in wit and in folklore. It compels us to pursue the inner meaning of the dream in these productions. But we must acknowledge that symbolism is not a result of the dream work, but is a peculiarity probably of our unconscious thinking, which furnishes to the dream work the matter for condensation, displacement, and dramatization.

◆◆◆

IV

DREAM ANALYSIS

Perhaps we shall now begin to suspect that dream interpretation is capable of giving us hints about the structure of our psychic apparatus which we have thus far expected in vain from philosophy. We shall not, however, follow this track, but return to our original problem as soon as we have cleared up the subject of dream-disfigurement. The question has arisen how dreams with disagreeable content can be analyzed as the fulfillment of wishes. We see now that this is possible in case dream-disfigurement has taken place, in case the disagreeable content serves only as a disguise for what is wished. Keeping in mind our assumptions in regard to the two psychic instances, we may now proceed to say: disagreeable dreams, as a matter of fact, contain something which is disagreeable to the second instance, but which at the same time fulfills a wish of the first instance. They are wish dreams in the sense that every dream originates in the first instance, while the second instance acts towards the dream only in repelling, not in a creative manner. If we limit ourselves to a consideration of what the second instance contributes to the dream, we can never understand the dream. If we do so, all the riddles which the authors have found in the dream remain unsolved.

That the dream actually has a secret meaning, which turns out to be the fulfillment of a wish, must be proved afresh for every case by means of an analysis. I therefore select several dreams which have painful contents and attempt an analysis of them. They are partly dreams of hysterical subjects, which require long preliminary

statements, and now and then also an examination of the psychic processes which occur in hysteria. I cannot, however, avoid this added difficulty in the exposition.

When I give a psychoneurotic patient analytical treatment, dreams are always, as I have said, the subject of our discussion. It must, therefore, give him all the psychological explanations through whose aid I myself have come to an understanding of his symptoms, and here I undergo an unsparing criticism, which is perhaps not less keen than that I must expect from my colleagues. Contradiction of the thesis that all dreams are the fulfillments of wishes is raised by my patients with perfect regularity. Here are several examples of the dream material which is offered me to refute this position.

"You always tell me that the dream is a wish fulfilled," begins a clever lady patient. "Now I shall tell you a dream in which the content is quite the opposite, in which a wish of mine is *not* fulfilled. How do you reconcile that with your theory? The dream is as follows:–

"I want to give a supper, but having nothing at hand except some smoked salmon, I think of going marketing, but I remember that it is Sunday afternoon, when all the shops are closed. I next try to telephone to some caterers, but the telephone is out of order.... Thus I must resign my wish to give a supper."

I answer, of course, that only the analysis can decide the meaning of this dream, although I admit that at first sight it seems sensible and coherent, and looks like the opposite of a wish-fulfillment. "But what occurrence has given rise to this dream?" I ask. "You know that the stimulus for a dream always lies among the experiences of the preceding day."

Analysis.–The husband of the patient, an upright and conscientious wholesale butcher, had told her the day before that he is growing too fat, and that he must, therefore, begin treatment for obesity. He was going to get up early, take exercise, keep to a strict diet, and above all accept no more invitations to suppers. She proceeds laughingly to relate how her husband at an inn table had made the acquaintance

of an artist, who insisted upon painting his portrait because he, the painter, had never found such an expressive head. But her husband had answered in his rough way, that he was very thankful for the honor, but that he was quite convinced that a portion of the backside of a pretty young girl would please the artist better than his whole face[5]. She said that she was at the time very much in love with her husband, and teased him a good deal. She had also asked him not to send her any caviare. What does that mean?

As a matter of fact, she had wanted for a long time to eat a caviare sandwich every forenoon, but had grudged herself the expense. Of course, she would at once get the caviare from her husband, as soon as she asked him for it. But she had begged him, on the contrary, not to send her the caviare, in order that she might tease him about it longer.

This explanation seems far-fetched to me. Unadmitted motives are in the habit of hiding behind such unsatisfactory explanations. We are reminded of subjects hypnotized by Bernheim, who carried out a posthypnotic order, and who, upon being asked for their motives, instead of answering: "I do not know why I did that," had to invent a reason that was obviously inadequate. Something similar is probably the case with the caviare of my patient. I see that she is compelled to create an unfulfilled wish in life. Her dream also shows the reproduction of the wish as accomplished. But why does she need an unfulfilled wish?

The ideas so far produced are insufficient for the interpretation of the dream. I beg for more. After a short pause, which corresponds to the overcoming of a resistance, she reports further that the day before she had made a visit to a friend, of whom she is really jealous, because her husband is always praising this woman so much. Fortunately, this friend is very lean and thin, and her husband likes well-rounded figures. Now of what did this lean friend speak? Naturally of her wish to become somewhat stouter. She also asked my patient: "When are you going to invite us again? You always have such a good table."

Now the meaning of the dream is clear. I may say to the patient:

---

5. To sit for the painter. Goethe: "And if he has no backside, how can the nobleman sit?"

"It is just as though you had thought at the time of the request: 'Of course, I'll invite you, so you can eat yourself fat at my house and become still more pleasing to my husband. I would rather give no more suppers.' The dream then tells you that you cannot give a supper, thereby fulfilling your wish not to contribute anything to the rounding out of your friend's figure. The resolution of your husband to refuse invitations to supper for the sake of getting thin teaches you that one grows fat on the things served in company." Now only some conversation is necessary to confirm the solution. The smoked salmon in the dream has not yet been traced. "How did the salmon mentioned in the dream occur to you?" "Smoked salmon is the favorite dish of this friend," she answered. I happen to know the lady, and may corroborate this by saying that she grudges herself the salmon just as much as my patient grudges herself the caviare.

The dream admits of still another and more exact interpretation, which is necessitated only by a subordinate circumstance. The two interpretations do not contradict one another, but rather cover each other and furnish a neat example of the usual ambiguity of dreams as well as of all other psychopathological formations. We have seen that at the same time that she dreams of the denial of the wish, the patient is in reality occupied in securing an unfulfilled wish (the caviare sandwiches). Her friend, too, had expressed a wish, namely, to get fatter, and it would not surprise us if our lady had dreamt that the wish of the friend was not being fulfilled. For it is her own wish that a wish of her friend's–for increase in weight–should not be fulfilled. Instead of this, however, she dreams that one of her own wishes is not fulfilled. The dream becomes capable of a new interpretation, if in the dream she does not intend herself, but her friend, if she has put herself in the place of her friend, or, as we may say, has identified herself with her friend.

I think she has actually done this, and as a sign of this identification she has created an unfulfilled wish in reality. But what is the meaning of this hysterical identification? To clear this up a thorough exposition is necessary. Identification is a highly important factor in the mechanism of hysterical symptoms; by this means patients

are enabled in their symptoms to represent not merely their own experiences, but the experiences of a great number of other persons, and can suffer, as it were, for a whole mass of people, and fill all the parts of a drama by means of their own personalities alone. It will here be objected that this is well-known hysterical imitation, the ability of hysteric subjects to copy all the symptoms which impress them when they occur in others, as though their pity were stimulated to the point of reproduction. But this only indicates the way in which the psychic process is discharged in hysterical imitation; the way in which a psychic act proceeds and the act itself are two different things. The latter is slightly more complicated than one is apt to imagine the imitation of hysterical subjects to be: it corresponds to an unconscious concluded process, as an example will show. The physician who has a female patient with a particular kind of twitching, lodged in the company of other patients in the same room of the hospital, is not surprised when some morning he learns that this peculiar hysterical attack has found imitations. He simply says to himself: The others have seen her and have done likewise: that is psychic infection. Yes, but psychic infection proceeds in somewhat the following manner: As a rule, patients know more about one another than the physician knows about each of them, and they are concerned about each other when the visit of the doctor is over. Some of them have an attack to-day: soon it is known among the rest that a letter from home, a return of lovesickness or the like, is the cause of it. Their sympathy is aroused, and the following syllogism, which does not reach consciousness, is completed in them: "If it is possible to have this kind of an attack from such causes, I too may have this kind of an attack, for I have the same reasons." If this were a cycle capable of becoming conscious, it would perhaps express itself in *fear* of getting the same attack; but it takes place in another psychic sphere, and, therefore, ends in the realization of the dreaded symptom. Identification is therefore not a simple imitation, but a sympathy based upon the same etiological claim; it expresses an "as though," and refers to some common quality which has remained in the unconscious.

Identification is most often used in hysteria to express sexual community. An hysterical woman identifies herself most readily—although not exclusively—with persons with whom she has had sexual relations, or who have sexual intercourse with the same persons as herself. Language takes such a conception into consideration: two lovers are "one." In the hysterical phantasy, as well as in the dream, it is sufficient for the identification if one thinks of sexual relations, whether or not they become real. The patient, then, only follows the rules of the hysterical thought processes when she gives expression to her jealousy of her friend (which, moreover, she herself admits to be unjustified, in that she puts herself in her place and identifies herself with her by creating a symptom—the denied wish). I might further clarify the process specifically as follows: She puts herself in the place of her friend in the dream, because her friend has taken her own place relation to her husband, and because she would like to take her friend's place in the esteem of her husband[6].

The contradiction to my theory of dreams in the case of another female patient, the most witty among all my dreamers, was solved in a simpler manner, although according to the scheme that the non-fulfillment of one wish signifies the fulfillment of another. I had one day explained to her that the dream is a wish of fulfillment. The next day she brought me a dream to the effect that she was traveling with her mother-in-law to their common summer resort. Now I knew that she had struggled violently against spending the summer in the neighborhood of her mother-in-law. I also knew that she had luckily avoided her mother-in-law by renting an estate in a far-distant country resort. Now the dream reversed this wished-for solution; was not this in the flattest contradiction to my theory of wish-fulfillment in the dream? Certainly, it was only necessary to draw the inferences from this dream in order to

6. I myself regret the introduction of such passages from the psychopathology of hysteria, which, because of their fragmentary representation and of being torn from all connection with the subject, cannot have a very enlightening influence. If these passages are capable of throwing light upon the intimate relations between the dream and the psychoneuroses, they have served the purpose for which I have taken them up.

get at its interpretation. According to this dream, I was in the wrong. *It was thus her wish that I should be in the wrong, and this wish the dream showed her as fulfilled.* But the wish that I should be in the wrong, which was fulfilled in the theme of the country home, referred to a more serious matter. At that time I had made up my mind, from the material furnished by her analysis, that something of significance for her illness must have occurred at a certain time in her life. She had denied it because it was not present in her memory. We soon came to see that I was in the right. Her wish that I should be in the wrong, which is transformed into the dream, thus corresponded to the justifiable wish that those things, which at the time had only been suspected, had never occurred at all.

Without an analysis, and merely by means of an assumption, I took the liberty of interpreting a little occurrence in the case of a friend, who had been my colleague through the eight classes of the Gymnasium. He once heard a lecture of mine delivered to a small assemblage, on the novel subject of the dream as the fulfillment of a wish. He went home, dreamt *that he had lost all his suits*—he was a lawyer—and then complained to me about it. I took refuge in the evasion: "One can't win all one's suits," but I thought to myself: "If for eight years I sat as Primus on the first bench, while he moved around somewhere in the middle of the class, may he not naturally have had a wish from his boyhood days that I, too, might for once completely disgrace myself?"

In the same way another dream of a more gloomy character was offered me by a female patient as a contradiction to my theory of the wish-dream. The patient, a young girl, began as follows: "You remember that my sister has now only one boy, Charles: she lost the elder one, Otto, while I was still at her house. Otto was my favorite; it was I who really brought him up. I like the other little fellow, too, but of course not nearly as much as the dead one. Now I dreamt last night that *I saw Charles lying dead before me. He was lying in his little coffin, his hands folded: there were candles all about, and, in short, it was just like the time of little Otto's death, which shocked me so profoundly*. Now tell me, what does this mean? You know me: am I really bad enough to wish my sister to lose the only child she has left? Or does the dream mean that I wish Charles to be dead rather than Otto, whom I like so much better?"

I assured her that this interpretation was impossible. After some reflection I was able to give her the interpretation of the dream, which I subsequently made her confirm.

Having become an orphan at an early age, the girl had been brought up in the house of a much older sister, and had met among the friends and visitors who came to the house, a man who made a lasting impression upon her heart. It looked for a time as though these barely expressed relations were to end in marriage, but this happy culmination was frustrated by the sister, whose motives have never found a complete explanation. After the break, the man who was loved by our patient avoided the house: she herself became independent some time after little Otto's death, to whom her affection had now turned. But she did not succeed in freeing herself from the inclination for her sister's friend in which she had become involved. Her pride commanded her to avoid him; but it was impossible for her to transfer her love to the other suitors who presented themselves in order. Whenever the man whom she loved, who was a member of the literary profession, announced a lecture anywhere, she was sure to be found in the audience; she also seized every other opportunity to see him from a distance unobserved by him. I remembered that on the day before she had told me that the Professor was going to a certain concert, and that she was also going there, in order to enjoy the sight of him. This was on the day of the dream; and the concert was to take place on the day on which she told me the dream. I could now easily see the correct interpretation, and I asked her whether she could think of any event which had happened after the death of little Otto. She answered immediately: "Certainly; at that time the Professor returned after a long absence, and I saw him once more beside the coffin of little Otto." It was exactly as I had expected. I interpreted the dream in the following manner: "If now the other boy were to die, the same thing would be repeated. You would spend the day with your sister, the Professor would surely come in order to offer condolence, and you would see him again under the same circumstances as at that time. The dream signifies nothing but this wish of yours to see him

again, against which you are fighting inwardly. I know that you are carrying the ticket for to-day's concert in your bag. Your dream is a dream of impatience; it has anticipated the meeting which is to take place to-day by several hours."

In order to disguise her wish she had obviously selected a situation in which wishes of that sort are commonly suppressed—a situation which is so filled with sorrow that love is not thought of. And yet, it is very easily probable that even in the actual situation at the bier of the second, more dearly loved boy, which the dream copied faithfully, she had not been able to suppress her feelings of affection for the visitor whom she had missed for so long a time.

A different explanation was found in the case of a similar dream of another female patient, who was distinguished in her earlier years by her quick wit and her cheerful demeanors and who still showed these qualities at least in the notion, which occurred to her in the course of treatment. In connection with a longer dream, it seemed to this lady that she saw her fifteen-year-old daughter lying dead before her in a box. She was strongly inclined to convert this dream-image into an objection to the theory of wish-fulfillment, but herself suspected that the detail of the box must lead to a different conception of the dream.[7] In the course of the analysis it occurred to her that on the evening before, the conversation of the company had turned upon the English word "box," and upon the numerous translations of it into German, such as box, theater box, chest, box on the ear, &c. From other components of the same dream it is now possible to add that the lady had guessed the relationship between the English word "box" and the German *Büchse*, and had then been haunted by the memory that *Büchse* (as well as "box") is used in vulgar speech to designate the female genital organ. It was therefore possible, making a certain allowance for her notions on the subject of topographical anatomy, to assume that the child in the box signified a child in the womb of the mother. At this stage of the explanation she no longer denied that the picture of the dream really corresponded to one of

7. Something like the smoked salmon in the dream of the deferred supper.

her wishes. Like so many other young women, she was by no means happy when she became pregnant, and admitted to me more than once the wish that her child might die before its birth; in a fit of anger following a violent scene with her husband she had even struck her abdomen with her fists in order to hit the child within. The dead child was, therefore, really the fulfillment of a wish, but a wish which had been put aside for fifteen years, and it is not surprising that the fulfillment of the wish was no longer recognized after so long an interval. For there had been many changes meanwhile.

The group of dreams to which the two last mentioned belong, having as content the death of beloved relatives, will be considered again under the head of "Typical Dreams." I shall there be able to show by new examples that in spite of their undesirable content, all these dreams must be interpreted as wish-fulfillments. For the following dream, which again was told me in order to deter me from a hasty generalization of the theory of wishing in dreams, I am indebted, not to a patient, but to an intelligent jurist of my acquaintance. "*I dream,*" my informant tells me, "*that I am walking in front of my house with a lady on my arm. Here a closed wagon is waiting, a gentleman steps up to me, gives his authority as an agent of the police, and demands that I should follow him. I only ask for time in which to arrange my affairs.* Can you possibly suppose this is a wish of mine to be arrested?" "Of course not," I must admit. "Do you happen to know upon what charge you were arrested?" "Yes; I believe for infanticide." "Infanticide? But you know that only a mother can commit this crime upon her newly born child?" "That is true."[8] "And under what circumstances did you dream; what happened on the evening before?" "I would rather not tell you that; it is a delicate matter." "But I must have it, otherwise we must forgo the interpretation of the dream." "Well, then, I will tell you. I spent the night, not at home, but at the house of a lady who means very much to me. When we awoke in the morning, something

---

8. It often happens that a dream is told incompletely, and that a recollection of the omitted portions appear only in the course of the analysis. These portions subsequently fitted in, regularly furnish the key to the interpretation. *Cf.* below, about forgetting in dreams.

again passed between us. Then I went to sleep again, and dreamt what I have told you." "The woman is married?" "Yes." "And you do not wish her to conceive a child?" "No; that might betray us." "Then you do not practice normal coitus?" "I take the precaution to withdraw before ejaculation." "Am I permitted to assume that you did this trick several times during the night, and that in the morning you were not quite sure whether you had succeeded?" "That might be the case." "Then your dream is the fulfillment of a wish. By means of it you secure the assurance that you have not begotten a child, or, what amounts to the same thing, that you have killed a child. I can easily demonstrate the connecting links. Do you remember, a few days ago we were talking about the distress of matrimony (Ehenot), and about the inconsistency of permitting the practice of coitus as long as no impregnation takes place, while every delinquency after the ovum and the semen meet and a fœtus is formed is punished as a crime? In connection with this, we also recalled the mediæval controversy about the moment of time at which the soul is really lodged in the fœtus, since the concept of murder becomes admissible only from that point on. Doubtless you also know the gruesome poem by Lenau, which puts infanticide and the prevention of children on the same plane." "Strangely enough, I had happened to think of Lenau during the afternoon." "Another echo of your dream. And now I shall demonstrate to you another subordinate wish-fulfillment in your dream. You walk in front of your house with the lady on your arm. So you take her home, instead of spending the night at her house, as you do in actuality. The fact that the wish-fulfillment, which is the essence of the dream, disguises itself in such an unpleasant form, has perhaps more than one reason. From my essay on the etiology of anxiety neuroses, you will see that I note interrupted coitus as one of the factors which cause the development of neurotic fear. It would be consistent with this that if after repeated cohabitation of the kind mentioned you should be left in an uncomfortable mood, which now becomes an element in the composition of your dream. You also make use of this unpleasant state of mind to conceal the wish-fulfillment. Furthermore, the mention of infanticide has not yet

been explained. Why does this crime, which is peculiar to females, occur to you?" "I shall confess to you that I was involved in such an affair years ago. Through my fault a girl tried to protect herself from the consequences of a *liaison* with me by securing an abortion. I had nothing to do with carrying out the plan, but I was naturally for a long time worried lest the affair might be discovered." "I understand; this recollection furnished a second reason why the supposition that you had done your trick badly must have been painful to you."

A young physician, who had heard this dream of my colleague when it was told, must have felt implicated by it, for he hastened to imitate it in a dream of his own, applying its mode of thinking to another subject. The day before he had handed in a declaration of his income, which was perfectly honest, because he had little to declare. He dreamt that an acquaintance of his came from a meeting of the tax commission and informed him that all the other declarations of income had passed uncontested, but that his own had awakened general suspicion, and that he would be punished with a heavy fine. The dream is a poorly-concealed fulfillment of the wish to be known as a physician with a large income. It likewise recalls the story of the young girl who was advised against accepting her suitor because he was a man of quick temper who would surely treat her to blows after they were married.

The answer of the girl was: "I wish he *would* strike me!" Her wish to be married is so strong that she takes into the bargain the discomfort which is said to be connected with matrimony, and which is predicted for her, and even raises it to a wish.

If I group the very frequently occurring dreams of this sort, which seem flatly to contradict my theory, in that they contain the denial of a wish or some occurrence decidedly unwished for, under the head of "counter wish-dreams," I observe that they may all be referred to two principles, of which one has not yet been mentioned, although it plays a large part in the dreams of human beings. One of the motives inspiring these dreams is the wish that I should appear in the wrong. These dreams regularly occur in the course of my treatment if the patient shows a resistance against me, and I can count with

a large degree of certainty upon causing such a dream after I have once explained to the patient my theory that the dream is a wish-fulfillment.[9] I may even expect this to be the case in a dream merely in order to fulfill the wish that I may appear in the wrong. The last dream which I shall tell from those occurring in the course of treatment again shows this very thing. A young girl who has struggled hard to continue my treatment, against the will of her relatives and the authorities whom she had consulted, dreams as follows: *She is forbidden at home to come to me any more. She then reminds me of the promise I made her to treat her for nothing if necessary, and I say to her: "I can show no consideration in money matters."*

It is not at all easy in this case to demonstrate the fulfillment of a wish, but in all cases of this kind there is a second problem, the solution of which helps also to solve the first. Where does she get the words which she puts into my mouth? Of course I have never told her anything like that, but one of her brothers, the very one who has the greatest influence over her, has been kind enough to make this remark about me. It is then the purpose of the dream that this brother should remain in the right; and she does not try to justify this brother merely in the dream; it is her purpose in life and the motive for her being ill.

The other motive for counter wish-dreams is so clear that there is danger of overlooking it, as for some time happened in my own case. In the sexual make-up of many people there is a masochistic component, which has arisen through the conversion of the aggressive, sadistic component into its opposite. Such people are called "ideal" masochists, if they seek pleasure not in the bodily pain which may be inflicted upon them, but in humiliation and in chastisement of the soul. It is obvious that such persons can have counter wish-dreams and disagreeable dreams, which, however, for them are nothing but wish-fulfillment, affording satisfaction for their masochistic inclinations.

9. Similar "counter wish-dreams" have been repeatedly reported to me within the last few years by my pupils who thus reacted to their first encounter with the "wish theory of the dream."

Here is such a dream. A young man, who has in earlier years tormented his elder brother, towards whom he was homosexually inclined, but who had undergone a complete change of character, has the following dream, which consists of three parts: (1) *He is "insulted" by his brother.* (2) *Two adults are caressing each other with homosexual intentions.* (3) *His brother has sold the enterprise whose management the young man reserved for his own future.* He awakens from the last-mentioned dream with the most unpleasant feelings, and yet it is a masochistic wish-dream, which might be translated: It would serve me quite right if my brother were to make that sale against my interest, as a punishment for all the torments which he has suffered at my hands.

I hope that the above discussion and examples will suffice–until further objection can be raised–to make it seem credible that even dreams with a painful content are to be analyzed as the fulfillments of wishes. Nor will it seem a matter of chance that in the course of interpretation one always happens upon subjects of which one does not like to speak or think. The disagreeable sensation which such dreams arouse is simply identical with the antipathy which endeavors–usually with success–to restrain us from the treatment or discussion of such subjects, and which must be overcome by all of us, if, in spite of its unpleasantness, we find it necessary to take the matter in hand. But this disagreeable sensation, which occurs also in dreams, does not preclude the existence of a wish; every one has wishes which he would not like to tell to others, which he does not want to admit even to himself. We are, on other grounds, justified in connecting the disagreeable character of all these dreams with the fact of dream disfigurement, and in concluding that these dreams are distorted, and that the wish-fulfillment in them is disguised until recognition is impossible for no other reason than that a repugnance, a will to suppress, exists in relation to the subject-matter of the dream or in relation to the wish which the dream creates. Dream disfigurement, then, turns out in reality to be an act of the censor. We shall take into consideration everything which the analysis of disagreeable dreams has brought to light if we reword our formula as follows: *The dream is the (disguised) fulfillment of a (suppressed, repressed) wish.*

Now there still remain as a particular species of dreams with painful content, dreams of anxiety, the inclusion of which under dreams of wishing will find least acceptance with the uninitiated. But I can settle the problem of anxiety dreams in very short order; for what they may reveal is not a new aspect of the dream problem; it is a question in their case of understanding neurotic anxiety in general. The fear which we experience in the dream is only seemingly explained by the dream content. If we subject the content of the dream to analysis, we become aware that the dream fear is no more justified by the dream content than the fear in a phobia is justified by the idea upon which the phobia depends. For example, it is true that it is possible to fall out of a window, and that some care must be exercised when one is near a window, but it is inexplicable why the anxiety in the corresponding phobia is so great, and why it follows its victims to an extent so much greater than is warranted by its origin. The same explanation, then, which applies to the phobia applies also to the dream of anxiety. In both cases the anxiety is only superficially attached to the idea which accompanies it and comes from another source.

On account of the intimate relation of dream fear to neurotic fear, discussion of the former obliges me to refer to the latter. In a little essay on "The Anxiety Neurosis,"[10] I maintained that neurotic fear has its origin in the sexual life, and corresponds to a libido which has been turned away from its object and has not succeeded in being applied. From this formula, which has since proved its validity more and more clearly, we may deduce the conclusion that the content of anxiety dreams is of a sexual nature, the libido belonging to which content has been transformed into fear.

◆◆◆

10. See *Selected Papers on Hysteria and other Psychoneuroses*, p. 133, translated by A.A. Brill, *Journal of Nervous and Mental Diseases*, Monograph Series.

V

SEX IN DREAMS

The more one is occupied with the solution of dreams, the more willing one must become to acknowledge that the majority of the dreams of adults treat of sexual material and give expression to erotic wishes. Only one who really analyzes dreams, that is to say, who pushes forward from their manifest content to the latent dream thoughts, can form an opinion on this subject—never the person who is satisfied with registering the manifest content (as, for example, Näcke in his works on sexual dreams). Let us recognize at once that this fact is not to be wondered at, but that it is in complete harmony with the fundamental assumptions of dream explanation. No other impulse has had to undergo so much suppression from the time of childhood as the sex impulse in its numerous components, from no other impulse have survived so many and such intense unconscious wishes, which now act in the sleeping state in such a manner as to produce dreams. In dream interpretation, this significance of sexual complexes must never be forgotten, nor must they, of course, be exaggerated to the point of being considered exclusive.

Of many dreams it can be ascertained by a careful interpretation that they are even to be taken bisexually, inasmuch as they result in an irrefutable secondary interpretation in which they realize homosexual feelings—that is, feelings that are common to the normal sexual activity of the dreaming person. But that all dreams are to be interpreted bisexually, seems to me to be a generalization as

indemonstrable as it is improbable, which I should not like to support. Above all I should not know how to dispose of the apparent fact that there are many dreams satisfying other than—in the widest sense—erotic needs, as dreams of hunger, thirst, convenience, &c. Likewise the similar assertions "that behind every dream one finds the death sentence" (Stekel), and that every dream shows "a continuation from the feminine to the masculine line" (Adler), seem to me to proceed far beyond what is admissible in the interpretation of dreams.

We have already asserted elsewhere that dreams which are conspicuously innocent invariably embody coarse erotic wishes, and we might confirm this by means of numerous fresh examples. But many dreams which appear indifferent, and which would never be suspected of any particular significance, can be traced back, after analysis, to unmistakably sexual wish-feelings, which are often of an unexpected nature. For example, who would suspect a sexual wish in the following dream until the interpretation had been worked out? The dreamer relates: *Between two stately palaces stands a little house, receding somewhat, whose doors are closed. My wife leads me a little way along the street up to the little house, and pushes in the door, and then I slip quickly and easily into the interior of a courtyard that slants obliquely upwards.*

Any one who has had experience in the translating of dreams will, of course, immediately perceive that penetrating into narrow spaces, and opening locked doors, belong to the commonest sexual symbolism, and will easily find in this dream a representation of attempted coition from behind (between the two stately buttocks of the female body). The narrow slanting passage is of course the vagina; the assistance attributed to the wife of the dreamer requires the interpretation that in reality it is only consideration for the wife which is responsible for the detention from such an attempt. Moreover, inquiry shows that on the previous day a young girl had entered the household of the dreamer who had pleased him, and who had given him the impression that she would not be altogether opposed to an approach of this sort. The little house between the two palaces is taken from a reminiscence of the Hradschin in Prague, and thus points again to the girl who is a native of that city.

If with my patients I emphasize the frequency of the Oedipus dream—of having sexual intercourse with one's mother—I get the answer: "I cannot remember such a dream." Immediately afterwards, however, there arises the recollection of another disguised and indifferent dream, which has been dreamed repeatedly by the patient, and the analysis shows it to be a dream of this same content—that is, another Oedipus dream. I can assure the reader that veiled dreams of sexual intercourse with the mother are a great deal more frequent than open ones to the same effect.

There are dreams about landscapes and localities in which emphasis is always laid upon the assurance: "I have been there before." In this case the locality is always the genital organ of the mother; it can indeed be asserted with such certainty of no other locality that one "has been there before."

A large number of dreams, often full of fear, which are concerned with passing through narrow spaces or with staying, in the water, are based upon fancies about the embryonic life, about the sojourn in the mother's womb, and about the act of birth. The following is the dream of a young man who in his fancy has already while in embryo taken advantage of his opportunity to spy upon an act of coition between his parents.

"He is in a deep shaft, in which there is a window, as in the Semmering Tunnel. At first he sees an empty landscape through this window, and then he composes a picture into it, which is immediately at hand and which fills out the empty space. The picture represents a field which is being thoroughly harrowed by an implement, and the delightful air, the accompanying idea of hard work, and the bluish-black clods of earth make a pleasant impression. He then goes on and sees a primary school opened ... and he is surprised that so much attention is devoted in it to the sexual feelings of the child, which makes him think of me."

Here is a pretty water-dream of a female patient, which was turned to extraordinary account in the course of treatment.

At her summer resort at the ... Lake, she hurls herself into the dark water at a place where the pale moon is reflected in the water.

Dreams of this sort are parturition dreams; their interpretation is accomplished by reversing the fact reported in the manifest dream content; thus, instead of "throwing one's self into the water," read "coming out of the water," that is, "being born." The place from which one is born is recognized if one thinks of the bad sense of the French "la lune." The pale moon thus becomes the white "bottom" (Popo), which the child soon recognizes as the place from which it came. Now what can be the meaning of the patient's wishing to be born at her summer resort? I asked the dreamer this, and she answered without hesitation: "Hasn't the treatment made me as though I were born again?" Thus the dream becomes an invitation to continue the cure at this summer resort, that is, to visit her there; perhaps it also contains a very bashful allusion to the wish to become a mother herself.[11]

Another dream of parturition, with its interpretation, I take from the work of E. Jones. *"She stood at the seashore watching a small boy, who seemed to be hers, wading into the water. This he did till the water covered him, and she could only see his head bobbing up and down near the surface. The scene then changed to the crowded hall of a hotel. Her husband left her, and she 'entered into conversation with' a stranger."* The second half of the dream was discovered in the analysis to represent a flight from her husband, and the entering into intimate relations with a third person, behind whom was plainly indicated Mr. X.'s brother mentioned in a former dream. The first part of the dream was a fairly evident birth phantasy. In dreams as in mythology, the delivery of a child *from* the uterine waters is commonly presented by distortion as the entry of the child *into* water; among many others, the births of Adonis, Osiris, Moses, and Bacchus are well-known

11. It is only of late that I have learned to value the significance of fancies and unconscious thoughts about life in the womb. They contain the explanation of the curious fear felt by so many people of being buried alive, as well as the profoundest unconscious reason for the belief in a life after death which represents nothing but a projection into the future of this mysterious life before birth. *The act of birth, moreover, is the first experience with fear, and is thus the source and model of the emotion of fear.*

illustrations of this. The bobbing up and down of the head in the water at once recalled to the patient the sensation of quickening she had experienced in her only pregnancy. Thinking of the boy going into the water induced a reverie in which she saw herself taking him out of the water, carrying him into the nursery, washing him and dressing him, and installing him in her household.

The second half of the dream, therefore, represents thoughts concerning the elopement, which belonged to the first half of the underlying latent content; the first half of the dream corresponded with the second half of the latent content, the birth phantasy. Besides this inversion in order, further inversions took place in each half of the dream. In the first half the child *entered* the water, and then his head bobbed; in the underlying dream thoughts first the quickening occurred, and then the child left the water (a double inversion). In the second half her husband left her; in the dream thoughts she left her husband.

Another parturition dream is related by Abraham of a young woman looking forward to her first confinement. From a place in the floor of the house a subterranean canal leads directly into the water (parturition path, amniotic liquor). She lifts up a trap in the floor, and there immediately appears a creature dressed in a brownish fur, which almost resembles a seal. This creature changes into the younger brother of the dreamer, to whom she has always stood in maternal relationship.

Dreams of "saving" are connected with parturition dreams. To save, especially to save from the water, is equivalent to giving birth when dreamed by a woman; this sense is, however, modified when the dreamer is a man.

Robbers, burglars at night, and ghosts, of which we are afraid before going to bed, and which occasionally even disturb our sleep, originate in one and the same childish reminiscence. They are the nightly visitors who have awakened the child to set it on the chamber so that it may not wet the bed, or have lifted the cover in order to see clearly how the child is holding its hands while sleeping. I have been able to induce an exact recollection of the nocturnal

visitor in the analysis of some of these anxiety dreams. The robbers were always the father, the ghosts more probably corresponded to feminine persons with white night-gowns.

When one has become familiar with the abundant use of symbolism for the representation of sexual material in dreams, one naturally raises the question whether there are not many of these symbols which appear once and for all with a firmly established significance like the signs in stenography; and one is tempted to compile a new dream-book according to the cipher method. In this connection it may be remarked that this symbolism does not belong peculiarly to the dream, but rather to unconscious thinking, particularly that of the masses, and it is to be found in greater perfection in the folklore, in the myths, legends, and manners of speech, in the proverbial sayings, and in the current witticisms of a nation than in its dreams.

The dream takes advantage of this symbolism in order to give a disguised representation to its latent thoughts. Among the symbols which are used in this manner there are of course many which regularly, or almost regularly, mean the same thing. Only it is necessary to keep in mind the curious plasticity of psychic material. Now and then a symbol in the dream content may have to be interpreted not symbolically, but according to its real meaning; at another time the dreamer, owing to a peculiar set of recollections, may create for himself the right to use anything whatever as a sexual symbol, though it is not ordinarily used in that way. Nor are the most frequently used sexual symbols unambiguous every time.

After these limitations and reservations I may call attention to the following: Emperor and Empress (King and Queen) in most cases really represent the parents of the dreamer; the dreamer himself or herself is the prince or princess. All elongated objects, sticks, tree-trunks, and umbrellas (on account of the stretching-up which might be compared to an erection! all elongated and sharp weapons, knives, daggers, and pikes, are intended to represent the male member. A frequent, not very intelligible, symbol for the same is a nail-file (on account of the rubbing and scraping?). Little cases, boxes, caskets,

closets, and stoves correspond to the female part. The symbolism of lock and key has been very gracefully employed by Uhland in his song about the "Grafen Eberstein," to make a common smutty joke. The dream of walking through a row of rooms is a brothel or harem dream. Staircases, ladders, and flights of stairs, or climbing on these, either upwards or downwards, are symbolic representations of the sexual act. Smooth walls over which one is climbing, façades of houses upon which one is letting oneself down, frequently under great anxiety, correspond to the erect human body, and probably repeat in the dream reminiscences of the upward climbing of little children on their parents or foster parents. "Smooth" walls are men. Often in a dream of anxiety one is holding on firmly to some projection from a house. Tables, set tables, and boards are women, perhaps on account of the opposition which does away with the bodily contours. Since "bed and board" (*mensa et thorus*) constitute marriage, the former are often put for the latter in the dream, and as far as practicable the sexual presentation complex is transposed to the eating complex. Of articles of dress the woman's hat may frequently be definitely interpreted as the male genital. In dreams of men one often finds the cravat as a symbol for the penis; this indeed is not only because cravats hang down long, and are characteristic of the man, but also because one can select them at pleasure, a freedom which is prohibited by nature in the original of the symbol. Persons who make use of this symbol in the dream are very extravagant with cravats, and possess regular collections of them. All complicated machines and apparatus in dream are very probably genitals, in the description of which dream symbolism shows itself to be as tireless as the activity of wit. Likewise many landscapes in dreams, especially with bridges or with wooded mountains, can be readily recognized as descriptions of the genitals. Finally where one finds incomprehensible neologisms one may think of combinations made up of components having a sexual significance. Children also in the dream often signify the genitals, as men and women are in the habit of fondly referring to their genital organ as their "little one." As a very recent symbol of the male genital may be mentioned the flying machine, utilization of which is justified by its

relation to flying as well as occasionally by its form. To play with a little child or to beat a little one is often the dream's representation of onanism. A number of other symbols, in part not sufficiently verified are given by Stekel, who illustrates them with examples. Right and left, according to him, are to be conceived in the dream in an ethical sense. "The right way always signifies the road to righteousness, the left the one to crime. Thus the left may signify homosexuality, incest, and perversion, while the right signifies marriage, relations with a prostitute, &c. The meaning is always determined by the individual moral view-point of the dreamer." Relatives in the dream generally play the rôle of genitals. Not to be able to catch up with a wagon is interpreted by Stekel as regret not to be able to come up to a difference in age. Baggage with which one travels is the burden of sin by which one is oppressed. Also numbers, which frequently occur in the dream, are assigned by Stekel a fixed symbolical meaning, but these interpretations seem neither sufficiently verified nor of general validity, although the interpretation in individual cases can generally be recognized as probable. In a recently published book by W. Stekel, *Die Sprache des Traumes*, which I was unable to utilize, there is a list of the most common sexual symbols, the object of which is to prove that all sexual symbols can be bisexually used. He states: "Is there a symbol which (if in any way permitted by the phantasy) may not be used simultaneously in the masculine and the feminine sense!" To be sure the clause in parentheses takes away much of the absoluteness of this assertion, for this is not at all permitted by the phantasy. I do not, however, think it superfluous to state that in my experience Stekel's general statement has to give way to the recognition of a greater manifoldness. Besides those symbols, which are just as frequent for the male as for the female genitals, there are others which preponderately, or almost exclusively, designate one of the sexes, and there are still others of which only the male or only the female signification is known. To use long, firm objects and weapons as symbols of the female genitals, or hollow objects (chests, pouches, &c.), as symbols of the male genitals, is indeed not allowed by the fancy.

It is true that the tendency of the dream and the unconscious fancy to utilize the sexual symbol bisexually betrays an archaic trend, for in childhood a difference in the genitals is unknown, and the same genitals are attributed to both sexes.

These very incomplete suggestions may suffice to stimulate others to make a more careful collection.

I shall now add a few examples of the application of such symbolisms in dreams, which will serve to show how impossible it becomes to interpret a dream without taking into account the symbolism of dreams, and how imperatively it obtrudes itself in many cases.

1. The hat as a symbol of the man (of the male genital): (a fragment from the dream of a young woman who suffered from agoraphobia on account of a fear of temptation).

"I am walking in the street in summer, I wear a straw hat of peculiar shape, the middle piece of which is bent upwards and the side pieces of which hang downwards (the description became here obstructed), and in such a fashion that one is lower than the other. I am cheerful and in a confidential mood, and as I pass a troop of young officers I think to myself: None of you can have any designs upon me."

As she could produce no associations to the hat, I said to her: "The hat is really a male genital, with its raised middle piece and the two downward hanging side pieces." I intentionally refrained from interpreting those details concerning the unequal downward hanging of the two side pieces, although just such individualities in the determinations lead the way to the interpretation. I continued by saying that if she only had a man with such a virile genital she would not have to fear the officers—that is, she would have nothing to wish from them, for she is mainly kept from going without protection and company by her fancies of temptation. This last explanation of her fear I had already been able to give her repeatedly on the basis of other material.

It is quite remarkable how the dreamer behaved after this interpretation. She withdrew her description of the hat, and claimed not to have said that the two side pieces were hanging downwards. I

was, however, too sure of what I had heard to allow myself to be misled, and I persisted in it. She was quiet for a while, and then found the courage to ask why it was that one of her husband's testicles was lower than the other, and whether it was the same in all men. With this the peculiar detail of the hat was explained, and the whole interpretation was accepted by her. The hat symbol was familiar to me long before the patient related this dream. From other but less transparent cases I believe that the hat may also be taken as a female genital.

2. The little one as the genital–to be run over as a symbol of sexual intercourse (another dream of the same agoraphobic patient).

"Her mother sends away her little daughter so that she must go alone. She rides with her mother to the railroad and sees her little one walking directly upon the tracks, so that she cannot avoid being run over. She hears the bones crackle. (From this she experiences a feeling of discomfort but no real horror.) She then looks out through the car window to see whether the parts cannot be seen behind. She then reproaches her mother for allowing the little one to go out alone." Analysis. It is not an easy matter to give here a complete interpretation of the dream. It forms part of a cycle of dreams, and can be fully understood only in connection with the others. For it is not easy to get the necessary material sufficiently isolated to prove the symbolism. The patient at first finds that the railroad journey is to be interpreted historically as an allusion to a departure from a sanatorium for nervous diseases, with the superintendent of which she naturally was in love. Her mother took her away from this place, and the physician came to the railroad station and handed her a bouquet of flowers on leaving; she felt uncomfortable because her mother witnessed this homage. Here the mother, therefore, appears as a disturber of her love affairs, which is the rôle actually played by this strict woman during her daughter's girlhood. The next thought referred to the sentence: "She then looks to see whether the parts can be seen behind." In the dream façade one would naturally be compelled to think of the parts of the little daughter run over and ground up. The thought, however, turns in quite a different direction. She recalls that she once saw her father in the bath-room naked from

behind; she then begins to talk about the sex differentiation, and asserts that in the man the genitals can be seen from behind, but in the woman they cannot. In this connection she now herself offers the interpretation that the little one is the genital, her little one (she has a four-year-old daughter) her own genital. She reproaches her mother for wanting her to live as though she had no genital, and recognizes this reproach in the introductory sentence of the dream; the mother sends away her little one so that she must go alone. In her phantasy going alone on the street signifies to have no man and no sexual relations (coire = to go together), and this she does not like. According to all her statements she really suffered as a girl on account of the jealousy of her mother, because she showed a preference for her father.

The "little one" has been noted as a symbol for the male or the female genitals by Stekel, who can refer in this connection to a very widespread usage of language.

The deeper interpretation of this dream depends upon another dream of the same night in which the dreamer identifies herself with her brother. She was a "tomboy," and was always being told that she should have been born a boy. This identification with the brother shows with special clearness that "the little one" signifies the genital. The mother threatened him (her) with castration, which could only be understood as a punishment for playing with the parts, and the identification, therefore, shows that she herself had masturbated as a child, though this fact she now retained only in memory concerning her brother. An early knowledge of the male genital which she later lost she must have acquired at that time according to the assertions of this second dream. Moreover the second dream points to the infantile sexual theory that girls originate from boys through castration. After I had told her of this childish belief, she at once confirmed it with an anecdote in which the boy asks the girl: "Was it cut off?" to which the girl replied, "No, it's always been so."

The sending away of the little one, of the genital, in the first dream therefore also refers to the threatened castration. Finally she blames her mother for not having been born a boy.

That "being run over" symbolizes sexual intercourse would not be evident from this dream if we were not sure of it from many other sources.

3. Representation of the genital by structures, stairways, and shafts. (Dream of a young man inhibited by a father complex.)

"He is taking a walk with his father in a place which is surely the Prater, for the *Rotunda* may be seen in front of which there is a small front structure to which is attached a captive balloon; the balloon, however, seems quite collapsed. His father asks him what this is all for; he is surprised at it, but he explains it to his father. They come into a court in which lies a large sheet of tin. His father wants to pull off a big piece of this, but first looks around to see if any one is watching. He tells his father that all he needs to do is to speak to the watchman, and then he can take without any further difficulty as much as he wants to. From this court a stairway leads down into a shaft, the walls of which are softly upholstered something like a leather pocketbook. At the end of this shaft there is a longer platform, and then a new shaft begins...."

Analysis. This dream belongs to a type of patient which is not favorable from a therapeutic point of view. They follow in the analysis without offering any resistances whatever up to a certain point, but from that point on they remain almost inaccessible. This dream he almost analyzed himself. "The Rotunda," he said, "is my genital, the captive balloon in front is my penis, about the weakness of which I have worried." We must, however, interpret in greater detail; the Rotunda is the buttock which is regularly associated by the child with the genital, the smaller front structure is the scrotum. In the dream his father asks him what this is all for—that is, he asks him about the purpose and arrangement of the genitals. It is quite evident that this state of affairs should be turned around, and that he should be the questioner. As such a questioning on the side of the father has never taken place in reality, we must conceive the dream thought as a wish, or take it conditionally, as follows: "If I had only asked my father for sexual enlightenment." The continuation of this thought we shall soon find in another place.

The court in which the tin sheet is spread out is not to be conceived symbolically in the first instance, but originates from his father's place of business. For discretionary reasons I have inserted the tin for another material in which the father deals, without, however, changing anything in the verbal expression of the dream. The dreamer had entered his father's business, and had taken a terrible dislike to the questionable practices upon which profit mainly depends. Hence the continuation of the above dream thought ("if I had only asked him") would be: "He would have deceived me just as he does his customers." For the pulling off, which serves to represent commercial dishonesty, the dreamer himself gives a second explanation–namely, onanism. This is not only entirely familiar to us, but agrees very well with the fact that the secrecy of onanism is expressed by its opposite ("Why one can do it quite openly"). It, moreover, agrees entirely with our expectations that the onanistic activity is again put off on the father, just as was the questioning in the first scene of the dream. The shaft he at once interprets as the vagina by referring to the soft upholstering of the walls. That the act of coition in the vagina is described as a going down instead of in the usual way as a going up, I have also found true in other instances[12].

The details that at the end of the first shaft there is a longer platform and then a new shaft, he himself explains biographically. He had for some time consorted with women sexually, but had then given it up because of inhibitions and now hopes to be able to take it up again with the aid of the treatment. The dream, however, becomes indistinct toward the end, and to the experienced interpreter it becomes evident that in the second scene of the dream the influence of another subject has begun to assert itself; in this his father's business and his dishonest practices signify the first vagina represented as a shaft so that one might think of a reference to the mother.

4. The male genital symbolized by persons and the female by a landscape.

(Dream of a woman of the lower class, whose husband is a policeman, reported by B. Dattner.)

---

12. Cf. *Zentralblatt für psychoanalyse*, I.

... Then some one broke into the house and anxiously called for a policeman. But he went with two tramps by mutual consent into a church,[13] to which led a great many stairs;[14] behind the church there was a mountain,[15] on top of which a dense forest.[16] The policeman was furnished with a helmet, a gorget, and a cloak.[17] The two vagrants, who went along with the policeman quite peaceably, had tied to their loins sack-like aprons.[18] A road led from the church to the mountain. This road was overgrown on each side with grass and brushwood, which became thicker and thicker as it reached the height of the mountain, where it spread out into quite a forest.

5. A stairway dream.

(Reported and interpreted by Otto Rank.)

For the following transparent pollution dream, I am indebted to the same colleague who furnished us with the dental-irritation dream.

"I am running down the stairway in the stair-house after a little girl, whom I wish to punish because she has done something to me. At the bottom of the stairs some one held the child for me. (A grown-up woman?) I grasp it, but do not know whether I have hit it, for I suddenly find myself in the middle of the stairway where I practice coitus with the child (in the air as it were). It is really no coitus, I only rub my genital on her external genital, and in doing this I see it very distinctly, as distinctly as I see her head which is lying sideways. During the sexual act I see hanging to the left and above me (also as if in the air) two small pictures, landscapes, representing a house on a green. On the smaller one my surname stood in the place where the painter's signature should be; it seemed to be intended for my birthday present.

13. Or chapel–vagina.
14. Symbol of coitus.
15. Mons veneris.
16. Crines pubis.
17. Demons in cloaks and capucines are, according to the explanation of a man versed in the subject, of a phallic nature.
18. The two halves of the scrotum.

A small sign hung in front of the pictures to the effect that cheaper pictures could also be obtained. I then see myself very indistinctly lying in bed, just as I had seen myself at the foot of the stairs, and I am awakened by a feeling of dampness which came from the pollution."

Interpretation. The dreamer had been in a book-store on the evening of the day of the dream, where, while he was waiting, he examined some pictures which were exhibited, which represented motives similar to the dream pictures. He stepped nearer to a small picture which particularly took his fancy in order to see the name of the artist, which, however, was quite unknown to him.

Later in the same evening, in company, he heard about a Bohemian servant-girl who boasted that her illegitimate child "was made on the stairs." The dreamer inquired about the details of this unusual occurrence, and learned that the servant-girl went with her lover to the home of her parents, where there was no opportunity for sexual relations, and that the excited man performed the act on the stairs. In witty allusion to the mischievous expression used about wine-adulterers, the dreamer remarked, "The child really grew on the cellar steps."

These experiences of the day, which are quite prominent in the dream content, were readily reproduced by the dreamer. But he just as readily reproduced an old fragment of infantile recollection which was also utilized by the dream. The stair-house was the house in which he had spent the greatest part of his childhood, and in which he had first become acquainted with sexual problems. In this house he used, among other things, to slide down the banister astride which caused him to become sexually excited. In the dream he also comes down the stairs very rapidly—so rapidly that, according to his own distinct assertions, he hardly touched the individual stairs, but rather "flew" or "slid down," as we used to say. Upon reference to this infantile experience, the beginning of the dream seems to represent the factor of sexual excitement. In the same house and in the adjacent residence the dreamer used to play pugnacious games with the neighboring children, in which he satisfied himself just as he did in the dream.

If one recalls from Freud's investigation of sexual symbolism[19] that in the dream stairs or climbing stairs almost regularly symbolizes coitus, the dream becomes clear. Its motive power as well as its effect, as is shown by the pollution, is of a purely libidinous nature. Sexual excitement became aroused during the sleeping state (in the dream this is represented by the rapid running or sliding down the stairs) and the sadistic thread in this is, on the basis of the pugnacious playing, indicated in the pursuing and overcoming of the child. The libidinous excitement becomes enhanced and urges to sexual action (represented in the dream by the grasping of the child and the conveyance of it to the middle of the stairway). Up to this point the dream would be one of pure, sexual symbolism, and obscure for the unpracticed dream interpreter. But this symbolic gratification, which would have insured undisturbed sleep, was not sufficient for the powerful libidinous excitement. The excitement leads to an orgasm, and thus the whole stairway symbolism is unmasked as a substitute for coitus. Freud lays stress on the rhythmical character of both actions as one of the reasons for the sexual utilization of the stairway symbolism, and this dream especially seems to corroborate this, for, according to the express assertion of the dreamer, the rhythm of a sexual act was the most pronounced feature in the whole dream.

Still another remark concerning the two pictures, which, aside from their real significance, also have the value of "Weibsbilder" (literally *woman-pictures*, but idiomatically *women*). This is at once shown by the fact that the dream deals with a big and a little picture, just as the dream content presents a big (grown up) and a little girl. That cheap pictures could also be obtained points to the prostitution complex, just as the dreamer's surname on the little picture and the thought that it was intended for his birthday, point to the parent complex (to be born on the stairway–to be conceived in coitus).

The indistinct final scene, in which the dreamer sees himself on the staircase landing lying in bed and feeling wet, seems to go back into childhood even beyond the infantile onanism, and manifestly has its prototype in similarly pleasurable scenes of bed-wetting.

---

19. See *Zentralblatt für Psychoanalyse*, vol. i., p. 2.

6. A modified stair-dream.

To one of my very nervous patients, who was an abstainer, whose fancy was fixed on his mother, and who repeatedly dreamed of climbing stairs accompanied by his mother, I once remarked that moderate masturbation would be less harmful to him than enforced abstinence. This influence provoked the following dream:

"His piano teacher reproaches him for neglecting his piano-playing, and for not practicing the *Etudes* of Moscheles and Clementi's *Gradus ad Parnassum.*" In relation to this he remarked that the *Gradus* is only a stairway, and that the piano itself is only a stairway as it has a scale.

It is correct to say that there is no series of associations which cannot be adapted to the representation of sexual facts. I conclude with the dream of a chemist, a young man, who has been trying to give up his habit of masturbation by replacing it with intercourse with women.

Preliminary statement.–On the day before the dream he had given a student instruction concerning Grignard's reaction, in which magnesium is to be dissolved in absolutely pure ether under the catalytic influence of iodine. Two days before, there had been an explosion in the course of the same reaction, in which the investigator had burned his hand.

Dream I. He is to make phenylmagnesium-bromid; he sees the apparatus with particular clearness, but he has substituted himself for the magnesium. He is now in a curious swaying attitude. He keeps repeating to himself, "This is the right thing, it is working, my feet are beginning to dissolve and my knees are getting soft." Then he reaches down and feels for his feet, and meanwhile (he does not know how) he takes his legs out of the crucible, and then again he says to himself, "That cannot be.... Yes, it must be so, it has been done correctly." Then he partially awakens, and repeats the dream to himself, because he wants to tell it to me. He is distinctly afraid of the analysis of the dream. He is much excited during this semi-sleeping state, and repeats continually, "Phenyl, phenyl."

II. He is in ....ing with his whole family; at half-past eleven. He is to be at the Schottenthor for a rendezvous with a certain lady, but he does not wake up until half-past eleven. He says to himself, "It is too late now; when you get there it will be half-past twelve." The next instant he sees the whole family gathered about the table—his mother and the servant girl with the soup-tureen with particular clearness. Then he says to himself, "Well, if we are eating already, I certainly can't get away."

Analysis: He feels sure that even the first dream contains a reference to the lady whom he is to meet at the rendezvous (the dream was dreamed during the night before the expected meeting). The student to whom he gave the instruction is a particularly unpleasant fellow; he had said to the chemist: "That isn't right," because the magnesium was still unaffected, and the latter answered as though he did not care anything about it: "It certainly isn't right." He himself must be this student; he is as indifferent towards his analysis as the student is towards his synthesis; the *He* in the dream, however, who accomplishes the operation, is myself. How unpleasant he must seem to me with his indifference towards the success achieved!

Moreover, he is the material with which the analysis (synthesis) is made. For it is a question of the success of the treatment. The legs in the dream recall an impression of the previous evening. He met a lady at a dancing lesson whom he wished to conquer; he pressed her to him so closely that she once cried out. After he had stopped pressing against her legs, he felt her firm responding pressure against his lower thighs as far as just above his knees, at the place mentioned in the dream. In this situation, then, the woman is the magnesium in the retort, which is at last working. He is feminine towards me, as he is masculine towards the woman. If it will work with the woman, the treatment will also work. Feeling and becoming aware of himself in the region of his knees refers to masturbation, and corresponds to his fatigue of the previous day.... The rendezvous had actually been set for half-past eleven. His wish to oversleep and to remain with his usual sexual objects (that is, with masturbation) corresponds with his resistance.

◆◆◆

VI

THE WISH IN DREAMS

That the dream should be nothing but a wish-fulfillment surely seemed strange to us all—and that not alone because of the contradictions offered by the anxiety dream.

After learning from the first analytical explanations that the dream conceals sense and psychic validity, we could hardly expect so simple a determination of this sense. According to the correct but concise definition of Aristotle, the dream is a continuation of thinking in sleep (in so far as one sleeps). Considering that during the day our thoughts produce such a diversity of psychic acts—judgments, conclusions, contradictions, expectations, intentions, &c.—why should our sleeping thoughts be forced to confine themselves to the production of wishes? Are there not, on the contrary, many dreams that present a different psychic act in dream form, *e.g.*, a solicitude, and is not the very transparent father's dream mentioned above of just such a nature? From the gleam of light falling into his eyes while asleep the father draws the solicitous conclusion that a candle has been upset and may have set fire to the corpse; he transforms this conclusion into a dream by investing it with a senseful situation enacted in the present tense. What part is played in this dream by the wish-fulfillment, and which are we to suspect—the predominance of the thought continued from, the waking state or of the thought incited by the new sensory impression?

All these considerations are just, and force us to enter more deeply into the part played by the wish-fulfillment in the dream, and into the significance of the waking thoughts continued in sleep.

It is in fact the wish-fulfillment that has already induced us to separate dreams into two groups. We have found some dreams that were plainly wish-fulfillments; and others in which wish-fulfillment could not be recognized, and was frequently concealed by every available means. In this latter class of dreams we recognized the influence of the dream censor. The undisguised wish dreams were chiefly found in children, yet fleeting open-hearted wish dreams *seemed* (I purposely emphasize this word) to occur also in adults.

We may now ask whence the wish fulfilled in the dream originates. But to what opposition or to what diversity do we refer this "whence"? I think it is to the opposition between conscious daily life and a psychic activity remaining unconscious which can only make itself noticeable during the night. I thus find a threefold possibility for the origin of a wish. Firstly, it may have been incited during the day, and owing to external circumstances failed to find gratification, there is thus left for the night an acknowledged but unfulfilled wish. Secondly, it may come to the surface during the day but be rejected, leaving an unfulfilled but suppressed wish. Or, thirdly, it may have no relation to daily life, and belong to those wishes that originate during the night from the suppression. If we now follow our scheme of the psychic apparatus, we can localize a wish of the first order in the system Forec. We may assume that a wish of the second order has been forced back from the Forec. system into the Unc. system, where alone, if anywhere, it can maintain itself; while a wish-feeling of the third order we consider altogether incapable of leaving the Unc. system. This brings up the question whether wishes arising from these different sources possess the same value for the dream, and whether they have the same power to incite a dream.

On reviewing the dreams which we have at our disposal for answering this question, we are at once moved to add as a fourth source of the dream-wish the actual wish incitements arising during

the night, such as thirst and sexual desire. It then becomes evident that the source of the dream-wish does not affect its capacity to incite a dream. That a wish suppressed during the day asserts itself in the dream can be shown by a great many examples. I shall mention a very simple example of this class. A somewhat sarcastic young lady, whose younger friend has become engaged to be married, is asked throughout the day by her acquaintances whether she knows and what she thinks of the fiancé. She answers with unqualified praise, thereby silencing her own judgment, as she would prefer to tell the truth, namely, that he is an ordinary person. The following night she dreams that the same question is put to her, and that she replies with the formula: "In case of subsequent orders it will suffice to mention the number." Finally, we have learned from numerous analyses that the wish in all dreams that have been subject to distortion has been derived from the unconscious, and has been unable to come to perception in the waking state. Thus it would appear that all wishes are of the same value and force for the dream formation.

I am at present unable to prove that the state of affairs is really different, but I am strongly inclined to assume a more stringent determination of the dream-wish. Children's dreams leave no doubt that an unfulfilled wish of the day may be the instigator of the dream. But we must not forget that it is, after all, the wish of a child, that it is a wish-feeling of infantile strength only. I have a strong doubt whether an unfulfilled wish from the day would suffice to create a dream in an adult. It would rather seem that as we learn to control our impulses by intellectual activity, we more and more reject as vain the formation or retention of such intense wishes as are natural to childhood. In this, indeed, there may be individual variations; some retain the infantile type of psychic processes longer than others. The differences are here the same as those found in the gradual decline of the originally distinct visual imagination.

In general, however, I am of the opinion that unfulfilled wishes of the day are insufficient to produce a dream in adults. I readily admit that the wish instigators originating in conscious like contribute

towards the incitement of dreams, but that is probably all. The dream would not originate if the foreconscious wish were not reinforced from another source.

That source is the unconscious. I believe that *the conscious wish is a dream inciter only if it succeeds in arousing a similar unconscious wish which reinforces it.* Following the suggestions obtained through the psychoanalysis of the neuroses, I believe that these unconscious wishes are always active and ready for expression whenever they find an opportunity to unite themselves with an emotion from conscious life, and that they transfer their greater intensity to the lesser intensity of the latter.[20] It may therefore seem that the conscious wish alone has been realized in a dream; but a slight peculiarity in the formation of this dream will put us on the track of the powerful helper from the unconscious. These ever active and, as it were, immortal wishes from the unconscious recall the legendary Titans who from time immemorial have borne the ponderous mountains which were once rolled upon them by the victorious gods, and which even now quiver from time to time from the convulsions of their mighty limbs; I say that these wishes found in the repression are of themselves of an infantile origin, as we have learned from the psychological investigation of the neuroses. I should like, therefore, to withdraw the opinion previously expressed that it is unimportant whence the dream-wish originates, and replace it by another, as follows: *The wish manifested in the dream must be an infantile one.* In the adult it originates in the Unc., while in the child, where no separation and censor as yet exist between Forec. and Unc., or where these are only in the process of formation, it is an unfulfilled

---

20. They share this character of indestructibility with all psychic acts that are really unconscious—that is, with psychic acts belonging to the system of the unconscious only. These paths are constantly open and never fall into disuse; they conduct the discharge of the exciting process as often as it becomes endowed with unconscious excitement To speak metaphorically they suffer the same form of annihilation as the shades of the lower region in the Odyssey, who awoke to new life the moment they drank blood. The processes depending on the foreconscious system are destructible in a different way. The psychotherapy of the neuroses is based on this difference.

and unrepressed wish from the waking state. I am aware that this conception cannot be generally demonstrated, but I maintain nevertheless that it can be frequently demonstrated, even when it was not suspected, and that it cannot be generally refuted.

The wish-feelings which remain from the conscious waking state are, therefore, relegated to the background in the dream formation. In the dream content I shall attribute to them only the part attributed to the material of actual sensations during sleep. If I now take into account those other psychic instigations remaining from the waking state which are not wishes, I shall only adhere to the line mapped out for me by this train of thought. We may succeed in provisionally terminating the sum of energy of our waking thoughts by deciding to go to sleep. He is a good sleeper who can do this; Napoleon I. is reputed to have been a model of this sort. But we do not always succeed in accomplishing it, or in accomplishing it perfectly. Unsolved problems, harassing cares, overwhelming impressions continue the thinking activity even during sleep, maintaining psychic processes in the system which we have termed the foreconscious. These mental processes continuing into sleep may be divided into the following groups: 1, That which has not been terminated during the day owing to casual prevention; 2, that which has been left unfinished by temporary paralysis of our mental power, *i.e.* the unsolved; 3, that which has been rejected and suppressed during the day. This unites with a powerful group (4) formed by that which has been excited in our Unc. during the day by the work of the foreconscious. Finally, we may add group (5) consisting of the indifferent and hence unsettled impressions of the day.

We should not underrate the psychic intensities introduced into sleep by these remnants of waking life, especially those emanating from the group of the unsolved. These excitations surely continue to strive for expression during the night, and we may assume with equal certainty that the sleeping state renders impossible the usual continuation of the excitement in the foreconscious and the termination of the excitement by its becoming conscious. As far as we can normally become conscious of our mental processes, even

during the night, in so far we are not asleep. I shall not venture to state what change is produced in the Forec. system by the sleeping state, but there is no doubt that the psychological character of sleep is essentially due to the change of energy in this very system, which also dominates the approach to motility, which is paralyzed during sleep. In contradistinction to this, there seems to be nothing in the psychology of the dream to warrant the assumption that sleep produces any but secondary changes in the conditions of the Unc. system. Hence, for the nocturnal excitation in the Force, there remains no other path than that followed by the wish excitements from the Unc. This excitation must seek reinforcement from the Unc., and follow the detours of the unconscious excitations. But what is the relation of the foreconscious day remnants to the dream? There is no doubt that they penetrate abundantly into the dream, that they utilize the dream content to obtrude themselves upon consciousness even during the night; indeed, they occasionally even dominate the dream content, and impel it to continue the work of the day; it is also certain that the day remnants may just as well have any other character as that of wishes; but it is highly instructive and even decisive for the theory of wish-fulfillment to see what conditions they must comply with in order to be received into the dream.

Let us pick out one of the dreams cited above as examples, *e.g.*, the dream in which my friend Otto seems to show the symptoms of Basedow's disease. My friend Otto's appearance occasioned me some concern during the day, and this worry, like everything else referring to this person, affected me. I may also assume that these feelings followed me into sleep. I was probably bent on finding out what was the matter with him. In the night my worry found expression in the dream which I have reported, the content of which was not only senseless, but failed to show any wish-fulfillment. But I began to investigate for the source of this incongruous expression of the solicitude felt during the day, and analysis revealed the connection. I identified my friend Otto with a certain Baron L. and myself with a Professor R. There was only one explanation for my being impelled

to select just this substitution for the day thought. I must have always been prepared in the Unc. to identify myself with Professor R., as it meant the realization of one of the immortal infantile wishes, viz. that of becoming great. Repulsive ideas respecting my friend, that would certainly have been repudiated in a waking state, took advantage of the opportunity to creep into the dream, but the worry of the day likewise found some form of expression through a substitution in the dream content. The day thought, which was no wish in itself but rather a worry, had in some way to find a connection with the infantile now unconscious and suppressed wish, which then allowed it, though already properly prepared, to "originate" for consciousness. The more dominating this worry, the stronger must be the connection to be established; between the contents of the wish and that of the worry there need be no connection, nor was there one in any of our examples.

We can now sharply define the significance of the unconscious wish for the dream. It may be admitted that there is a whole class of dreams in which the incitement originates preponderatingly or even exclusively from the remnants of daily life; and I believe that even my cherished desire to become at some future time a "professor extraordinarius" would have allowed me to slumber undisturbed that night had not my worry about my friend's health been still active. But this worry alone would not have produced a dream; the motive power needed by the dream had to be contributed by a wish, and it was the affair of the worriment to procure for itself such wish as a motive power of the dream. To speak figuratively, it is quite possible that a day thought plays the part of the contractor (*entrepreneur*) in the dream. But it is known that no matter what idea the contractor may have in mind, and how desirous he may be of putting it into operation, he can do nothing without capital; he must depend upon a capitalist to defray the necessary expenses, and this capitalist, who supplies the psychic expenditure for the dream is invariably and indisputably *a wish from the unconscious*, no matter what the nature of the waking thought may be.

In other cases the capitalist himself is the contractor for the dream; this, indeed, seems to be the more usual case. An unconscious wish is produced by the day's work, which in turn creates the dream. The dream processes, moreover, run parallel with all the other possibilities of the economic relationship used here as an illustration. Thus, the entrepreneur may contribute some capital himself, or several entrepreneurs may seek the aid of the same capitalist, or several capitalists may jointly supply the capital required by the entrepreneur. Thus there are dreams produced by more than one dream-wish, and many similar variations which may readily be passed over and are of no further interest to us. What we have left unfinished in this discussion of the dream-wish we shall be able to develop later.

The "tertium comparationis" in the comparisons just employed—*i.e.* the sum placed at our free disposal in proper allotment—admits of still finer application for the illustration of the dream structure. We can recognize in most dreams a center especially supplied with perceptible intensity. This is regularly the direct representation of the wish-fulfillment; for, if we undo the displacements of the dream-work by a process of retrogression, we find that the psychic intensity of the elements in the dream thoughts is replaced by the perceptible intensity of the elements in the dream content. The elements adjoining the wish-fulfillment have frequently nothing to do with its sense, but prove to be descendants of painful thoughts which oppose the wish. But, owing to their frequently artificial connection with the central element, they have acquired sufficient intensity to enable them to come to expression. Thus, the force of expression of the wish-fulfillment is diffused over a certain sphere of association, within which it raises to expression all elements, including those that are in themselves impotent. In dreams having several strong wishes we can readily separate from one another the spheres of the individual wish-fulfillments; the gaps in the dream likewise can often be explained as boundary zones.

Although the foregoing remarks have considerably limited the significance of the day remnants for the dream, it will nevertheless be worth our while to give them some attention. For they must be a necessary ingredient in the formation of the dream, inasmuch as

experience reveals the surprising fact that every dream shows in its content a connection with some impression of a recent day, often of the most indifferent kind. So far we have failed to see any necessity for this addition to the dream mixture. This necessity appears only when we follow closely the part played by the unconscious wish, and then seek information in the psychology of the neuroses. We thus learn that the unconscious idea, as such, is altogether incapable of entering into the foreconscious, and that it can exert an influence there only by uniting with a harmless idea already belonging to the foreconscious, to which it transfers its intensity and under which it allows itself to be concealed. This is the fact of transference which furnishes an explanation for so many surprising occurrences in the psychic life of neurotics.

The idea from the foreconscious which thus obtains an unmerited abundance of intensity may be left unchanged by the transference, or it may have forced upon it a modification from the content of the transferring idea. I trust the reader will pardon my fondness for comparisons from daily life, but I feel tempted to say that the relations existing for the repressed idea are similar to the situations existing in Austria for the American dentist, who is forbidden to practise unless he gets permission from a regular physician to use his name on the public signboard and thus cover the legal requirements. Moreover, just as it is naturally not the busiest physicians who form such alliances with dental practitioners, so in the psychic life only such foreconscious or conscious ideas are chosen to cover a repressed idea as have not themselves attracted much of the attention which is operative in the foreconscious. The unconscious entangles with its connections preferentially either those impressions and ideas of the foreconscious which have been left unnoticed as indifferent, or those that have soon been deprived of this attention through rejection. It is a familiar fact from the association studies confirmed by every experience, that ideas which have formed intimate connections in one direction assume an almost negative attitude to whole groups of new connections. I once tried from this principle to develop a theory for hysterical paralysis.

If we assume that the same need for the transference of the repressed ideas which we have learned to know from the analysis of the neuroses makes its influence felt in the dream as well, we can at once explain two riddles of the dream, viz. that every dream analysis shows an interweaving of a recent impression, and that this recent element is frequently of the most indifferent character. We may add what we have already learned elsewhere, that these recent and indifferent elements come so frequently into the dream content as a substitute for the most deep-lying of the dream thoughts, for the further reason that they have least to fear from the resisting censor. But while this freedom from censorship explains only the preference for trivial elements, the constant presence of recent elements points to the fact that there is a need for transference. Both groups of impressions satisfy the demand of the repression for material still free from associations, the indifferent ones because they have offered no inducement for extensive associations, and the recent ones because they have had insufficient time to form such associations.

We thus see that the day remnants, among which we may now include the indifferent impressions when they participate in the dream formation, not only borrow from the Unc. the motive power at the disposal of the repressed wish, but also offer to the unconscious something indispensable, namely, the attachment necessary to the transference. If we here attempted to penetrate more deeply into the psychic processes, we should first have to throw more light on the play of emotions between the foreconscious and the unconscious, to which, indeed, we are urged by the study of the psychoneuroses, whereas the dream itself offers no assistance in this respect.

Just one further remark about the day remnants. There is no doubt that they are the actual disturbers of sleep, and not the dream, which, on the contrary, strives to guard sleep. But we shall return to this point later.

We have so far discussed the dream-wish, we have traced it to the sphere of the Unc., and analyzed its relations to the day remnants, which in turn may be either wishes, psychic emotions of any other kind, or simply recent impressions. We have thus made room for any

claims that may be made for the importance of conscious thought activity in dream formations in all its variations. Relying upon our thought series, it would not be at all impossible for us to explain even those extreme cases in which the dream as a continuer of the day work brings to a happy conclusion and unsolved problem possess an example, the analysis of which might reveal the infantile or repressed wish source furnishing such alliance and successful strengthening of the efforts of the foreconscious activity. But we have not come one step nearer a solution of the riddle: Why can the unconscious furnish the motive power for the wish-fulfillment only during sleep? The answer to this question must throw light on the psychic nature of wishes; and it will be given with the aid of the diagram of the psychic apparatus.

We do not doubt that even this apparatus attained its present perfection through a long course of development. Let us attempt to restore it as it existed in an early phase of its activity. From assumptions, to be confirmed elsewhere, we know that at first the apparatus strove to keep as free from excitement as possible, and in its first formation, therefore, the schème took the form of a reflex apparatus, which enabled it promptly to discharge through the motor tracts any sensible stimulus reaching it from without. But this simple function was disturbed by the wants of life, which likewise furnish the impulse for the further development of the apparatus. The wants of life first manifested themselves to it in the form of the great physical needs. The excitement aroused by the inner want seeks an outlet in motility, which may be designated as "inner changes" or as an "expression of the emotions." The hungry child cries or fidgets helplessly, but its situation remains unchanged; for the excitation proceeding from an inner want requires, not a momentary outbreak, but a force working continuously. A change can occur only if in some way a feeling of gratification is experienced–which in the case of the child must be through outside help–in order to remove the inner excitement. An essential constituent of this experience is the appearance of a certain perception (of food in our example), the memory picture of which thereafter remains associated with the memory trace of the excitation of want.

Thanks to the established connection, there results at the next appearance of this want a psychic feeling which revives the memory picture of the former perception, and thus recalls the former perception itself, *i.e.* it actually re-establishes the situation of the first gratification. We call such a feeling a wish; the reappearance of the perception constitutes the wish-fulfillment, and the full revival of the perception by the want excitement constitutes the shortest road to the wish-fulfillment. We may assume a primitive condition of the psychic apparatus in which this road is really followed, *i.e.* where the wishing merges into an hallucination, This first psychic activity therefore aims at an identity of perception, *i.e.* it aims at a repetition of that perception which is connected with the fulfillment of the want.

This primitive mental activity must have been modified by bitter practical experience into a more expedient secondary activity. The establishment of the identity perception on the short regressive road within the apparatus does not in another respect carry with it the result which inevitably follows the revival of the same perception from without. The gratification does not take place, and the want continues. In order to equalize the internal with the external sum of energy, the former must be continually maintained, just as actually happens in the hallucinatory psychoses and in the deliriums of hunger which exhaust their psychic capacity in clinging to the object desired. In order to make more appropriate use of the psychic force, it becomes necessary to inhibit the full regression so as to prevent it from extending beyond the image of memory, whence it can select other paths leading ultimately to the establishment of the desired identity from the outer world. This inhibition and consequent deviation from the excitation becomes the task of a second system which dominates the voluntary motility, *i.e.* through whose activity the expenditure of motility is now devoted to previously recalled purposes. But this entire complicated mental activity which works its way from the memory picture to the establishment of the perception identity from the outer world merely represents a detour which has

been forced upon the wish-fulfillment by experience.[21] Thinking is indeed nothing but the equivalent of the hallucinatory wish; and if the dream be called a wish-fulfillment this becomes self-evident, as nothing but a wish can impel our psychic apparatus to activity. The dream, which in fulfilling its wishes follows the short regressive path, thereby preserves for us only an example of the primary form of the psychic apparatus which has been abandoned as inexpedient. What once ruled in the waking state when the psychic life was still young and unfit seems to have been banished into the sleeping state, just as we see again in the nursery the bow and arrow, the discarded primitive weapons of grown-up humanity. *The dream is a fragment of the abandoned psychic life of the child.* In the psychoses these modes of operation of the psychic apparatus, which are normally suppressed in the waking state, reassert themselves, and then betray their inability to satisfy our wants in the outer world.

The unconscious wish-feelings evidently strive to assert themselves during the day also, and the fact of transference and the psychoses teach us that they endeavor to penetrate to consciousness and dominate motility by the road leading through the system of the foreconscious. It is, therefore, the censor lying between the Unc. and the Forec., the assumption of which is forced upon us by the dream, that we have to recognize and honor as the guardian of our psychic health. But is it not carelessness on the part of this guardian to diminish its vigilance during the night and to allow the suppressed emotions of the Unc. to come to expression, thus again making possible the hallucinatory regression? I think not, for when the critical guardian goes to rest—and we have proof that his slumber is not profound—he takes care to close the gate to motility. No matter what feelings from the otherwise inhibited Unc. may roam about on the scene, they need not be interfered with; they remain harmless because they are unable to put in motion the motor apparatus which alone can exert a modifying

---

21. Le Lorrain justly extols the wish-fulfilment of the dream: "Sans fatigue sérieuse, sans être obligé de recourir à cette lutte opinâtre et longue qui use et corrode les jouissances poursuivies."

influence upon the outer world. Sleep guarantees the security of the fortress which is under guard. Conditions are less harmless when a displacement of forces is produced, not through a nocturnal diminution in the operation of the critical censor, but through pathological enfeeblement of the latter or through pathological reinforcement of the unconscious excitations, and this while the foreconscious is charged with energy and the avenues to motility are open. The guardian is then overpowered, the unconscious excitations subdue the Forec.; through it they dominate our speech and actions, or they enforce the hallucinatory regression, thus governing an apparatus not designed for them by virtue of the attraction exerted by the perceptions on the distribution of our psychic energy. We call this condition a psychosis.

We are now in the best position to complete our psychological construction, which has been interrupted by the introduction of the two systems, Unc. and Forec. We have still, however, ample reason for giving further consideration to the wish as the sole psychic motive power in the dream. We have explained that the reason why the dream is in every case a wish realization is because it is a product of the Unc., which knows no other aim in its activity but the fulfillment of wishes, and which has no other forces at its disposal but wish-feelings. If we avail ourselves for a moment longer of the right to elaborate from the dream interpretation such far-reaching psychological speculations, we are in duty bound to demonstrate that we are thereby bringing the dream into a relationship which may also comprise other psychic structures. If there exists a system of the Unc.—or something sufficiently analogous to it for the purpose of our discussion—the dream cannot be its sole manifestation; every dream may be a wish-fulfillment, but there must be other forms of abnormal wish-fulfillment beside this of dreams. Indeed, the theory of all psychoneurotic symptoms culminates in the proposition *that they too must be taken as wish-fulfillments of the unconscious*. Our explanation makes the dream only the first member of a group most important for the psychiatrist, an understanding of which means the solution of the purely psychological part of the psychiatric problem. But

other members of this group of wish-fulfillments, *e.g.*, the hysterical symptoms, evince one essential quality which I have so far failed to find in the dream. Thus, from the investigations frequently referred to in this treatise, I know that the formation of an hysterical symptom necessitates the combination of both streams of our psychic life. The symptom is not merely the expression of a realized unconscious wish, but it must be joined by another wish from the foreconscious which is fulfilled by the same symptom; so that the symptom is at least doubly determined, once by each one of the conflicting systems. Just as in the dream, there is no limit to further over-determination. The determination not derived from the Unc. is, as far as I can see, invariably a stream of thought in reaction against the unconscious wish, *e.g.*, a self-punishment. Hence I may say, in general, that *an hysterical symptom originates only where two contrasting wish-fulfillments, having their source in different psychic systems, are able to combine in one expression.* (Compare my latest formulation of the origin of the hysterical symptoms in a treatise published by the *Zeitschrift für Sexualwissenschaft*, by Hirschfeld and others, 1908). Examples on this point would prove of little value, as nothing but a complete unveiling of the complication in question would carry conviction. I therefore content myself with the mere assertion, and will cite an example, not for conviction but for explication. The hysterical vomiting of a female patient proved, on the one hand, to be the realization of an unconscious fancy from the time of puberty, that she might be continuously pregnant and have a multitude of children, and this was subsequently united with the wish that she might have them from as many men as possible. Against this immoderate wish there arose a powerful defensive impulse. But as the vomiting might spoil the patient's figure and beauty, so that she would not find favor in the eyes of mankind, the symptom was therefore in keeping with her punitive trend of thought, and, being thus admissible from both sides, it was allowed to become a reality. This is the same manner of consenting to a wish-fulfillment which the queen of the Parthians chose for the triumvir Crassus. Believing that he had undertaken the campaign out of greed for gold, she caused molten gold to be poured into the throat of

the corpse. "Now hast thou what thou hast longed for." As yet we know of the dream only that it expresses a wish-fulfillment of the unconscious; and apparently the dominating foreconscious permits this only after it has subjected the wish to some distortions. We are really in no position to demonstrate regularly a stream of thought antagonistic to the dream-wish which is realized in the dream as in its counterpart. Only now and then have we found in the dream traces of reaction formations, as, for instance, the tenderness toward friend R. in the "uncle dream." But the contribution from the foreconscious, which is missing here, may be found in another place. While the dominating system has withdrawn on the wish to sleep, the dream may bring to expression with manifold distortions a wish from the Unc., and realize this wish by producing the necessary changes of energy in the psychic apparatus, and may finally retain it through the entire duration of sleep.[22]

This persistent wish to sleep on the part of the foreconscious in general facilitates the formation of the dream. Let us refer to the dream of the father who, by the gleam of light from the death chamber, was brought to the conclusion that the body has been set on fire. We have shown that one of the psychic forces decisive in causing the father to form this conclusion, instead of being awakened by the gleam of light, was the wish to prolong the life of the child seen in the dream by one moment. Other wishes proceeding from the repression probably escape us, because we are unable to analyze this dream. But as a second motive power of the dream we may mention the father's desire to sleep, for, like the life of the child, the sleep of the father is prolonged for a moment by the dream. The underlying motive is: "Let the dream go on, otherwise I must wake up." As in this dream so also in all other dreams, the wish to sleep lends its support to the unconscious wish. We reported dreams which were apparently dreams of convenience. But, properly speaking, all dreams may claim this designation. The efficacy of the wish to continue to sleep is the most easily recognized

22. This idea has been borrowed from The Theory of Sleep by Liébault, who revived hypnotic investigation in our days. (Du Sommeil provoqué, etc.; Paris, 1889.)

in the waking dreams, which so transform the objective sensory stimulus as to render it compatible with the continuance of sleep; they interweave this stimulus with the dream in order to rob it of any claims it might make as a warning to the outer world. But this wish to continue to sleep must also participate in the formation of all other dreams which may disturb the sleeping state from within only. "Now, then, sleep on; why, it's but a dream"; this is in many cases the suggestion of the Forec. to consciousness when the dream goes too far; and this also describes in a general way the attitude of our dominating psychic activity toward dreaming, though the thought remains tacit. I must draw the conclusion that *throughout our entire sleeping state we are just as certain that we are dreaming as we are certain that we are sleeping.* We are compelled to disregard the objection urged against this conclusion that our consciousness is never directed to a knowledge of the former, and that it is directed to a knowledge of the latter only on special occasions when the censor is unexpectedly surprised. Against this objection we may say that there are persons who are entirely conscious of their sleeping and dreaming, and who are apparently endowed with the conscious faculty of guiding their dream life. Such a dreamer, when dissatisfied with the course taken by the dream, breaks it off without awakening, and begins it anew in order to continue it with a different turn, like the popular author who, on request, gives a happier ending to his play. Or, at another time, if placed by the dream in a sexually exciting situation, he thinks in his sleep: "I do not care to continue this dream and exhaust myself by a pollution; I prefer to defer it in favor of a real situation."

◆◆◆

VII

THE FUNCTION OF THE DREAM

Since we know that the foreconscious is suspended during the night by the wish to sleep, we can proceed to an intelligent investigation of the dream process. But let us first sum up the knowledge of this process already gained. We have shown that the waking activity leaves day remnants from which the sum of energy cannot be entirely removed; or the waking activity revives during the day one of the unconscious wishes; or both conditions occur simultaneously; we have already discovered the many variations that may take place. The unconscious wish has already made its way to the day remnants, either during the day or at any rate with the beginning of sleep, and has effected a transference to it. This produces a wish transferred to the recent material, or the suppressed recent wish comes to life again through a reinforcement from the unconscious. This wish now endeavors to make its way to consciousness on the normal path of the mental processes through the foreconscious, to which indeed it belongs through one of its constituent elements. It is confronted, however, by the censor, which is still active, and to the influence of which it now succumbs. It now takes on the distortion for which the way has already been paved by its transference to the recent material. Thus far it is in the way of becoming something resembling an obsession, delusion, or the like, *i.e.* a thought reinforced by a transference and distorted in expression by the censor. But its further progress is now checked through the dormant state of the foreconscious; this system has apparently protected itself against invasion by diminishing its excitements. The dream process,

therefore, takes the regressive course, which has just been opened by the peculiarity of the sleeping state, and thereby follows the attraction exerted on it by the memory groups, which themselves exist in part only as visual energy not yet translated into terms of the later systems. On its way to regression the dream takes on the form of dramatization. The subject of compression will be discussed later. The dream process has now terminated the second part of its repeatedly impeded course. The first part expended itself progressively from the unconscious scenes or phantasies to the foreconscious, while the second part gravitates from the advent of the censor back to the perceptions. But when the dream process becomes a content of perception it has, so to speak, eluded the obstacle set up in the Forec. by the censor and by the sleeping state. It succeeds in drawing attention to itself and in being noticed by consciousness. For consciousness, which means to us a sensory organ for the reception of psychic qualities, may receive stimuli from two sources–first, from the periphery of the entire apparatus, viz. from the perception system, and, secondly, from the pleasure and pain stimuli, which constitute the sole psychic quality produced in the transformation of energy within the apparatus. All other processes in the system, even those in the foreconscious, are devoid of any psychic quality, and are therefore not objects of consciousness inasmuch as they do not furnish pleasure or pain for perception. We shall have to assume that those liberations of pleasure and pain automatically regulate the outlet of the occupation processes. But in order to make possible more delicate functions, it was later found necessary to render the course of the presentations more independent of the manifestations of pain. To accomplish this the Forec. system needed some qualities of its own which could attract consciousness, and most probably received them through the connection of the foreconscious processes with the memory system of the signs of speech, which is not devoid of qualities. Through the qualities of this system, consciousness, which had hitherto been a sensory organ only for the perceptions, now becomes also a sensory organ for a part of our mental processes. Thus we have now, as it were, two sensory surfaces, one directed to perceptions and the other to the foreconscious mental processes.

I must assume that the sensory surface of consciousness devoted to the Forec. is rendered less excitable by sleep than that directed to the P-systems. The giving up of interest for the nocturnal mental processes is indeed purposeful. Nothing is to disturb the mind; the Forec. wants to sleep. But once the dream becomes a perception, it is then capable of exciting consciousness through the qualities thus gained. The sensory stimulus accomplishes what it was really destined for, namely, it directs a part of the energy at the disposal of the Forec. in the form of attention upon the stimulant. We must, therefore, admit that the dream invariably awakens us, that is, it puts into activity a part of the dormant force of the Forec. This force imparts to the dream that influence which we have designated as secondary elaboration for the sake of connection and comprehensibility. This means that the dream is treated by it like any other content of perception; it is subjected to the same ideas of expectation, as far at least as the material admits. As far as the direction is concerned in this third part of the dream, it may be said that here again the movement is progressive.

To avoid misunderstanding, it will not be amiss to say a few words about the temporal peculiarities of these dream processes. In a very interesting discussion, apparently suggested by Maury's puzzling guillotine dream, Goblet tries to demonstrate that the dream requires no other time than the transition period between sleeping and awakening. The awakening requires time, as the dream takes place during that period. One is inclined to believe that the final picture of the dream is so strong that it forces the dreamer to awaken; but, as a matter of fact, this picture is strong only because the dreamer is already very near awakening when it appears. "Un rêve c'est un réveil qui commence."

It has already been emphasized by Dugas that Goblet was forced to repudiate many facts in order to generalize his theory. There are, moreover, dreams from which we do not awaken, *e.g.*, some dreams in which we dream that we dream. From our knowledge of the dream-work, we can by no means admit that it extends only over the period of awakening. On the contrary, we must consider it probable that the first part of the dream-work begins during the day when we are still under the domination of the foreconscious. The second phase of the

dream-work, viz. the modification through the censor, the attraction by the unconscious scenes, and the penetration to perception must continue throughout the night. And we are probably always right when we assert that we feel as though we had been dreaming the whole night, although we cannot say what. I do not, however, think it necessary to assume that, up to the time of becoming conscious, the dream processes really follow the temporal sequence which we have described, viz. that there is first the transferred dream-wish, then the distortion of the censor, and consequently the change of direction to regression, and so on. We were forced to form such a succession for the sake of *description*; in reality, however, it is much rather a matter of simultaneously trying this path and that, and of emotions fluctuating to and fro, until finally, owing to the most expedient distribution, one particular grouping is secured which remains. From certain personal experiences, I am myself inclined to believe that the dream-work often requires more than one day and one night to produce its result; if this be true, the extraordinary art manifested in the construction of the dream loses all its marvels. In my opinion, even the regard for comprehensibility as an occurrence of perception may take effect before the dream attracts consciousness to itself. To be sure, from now on the process is accelerated, as the dream is henceforth subjected to the same treatment as any other perception. It is like fireworks, which require hours of preparation and only a moment for ignition.

Through the dream-work the dream process now gains either sufficient intensity to attract consciousness to itself and arouse the foreconscious, which is quite independent of the time or profundity of sleep, or, its intensity being insufficient it must wait until it meets the attention which is set in motion immediately before awakening. Most dreams seem to operate with relatively slight psychic intensities, for they wait for the awakening. This, however, explains the fact that we regularly perceive something dreamt on being suddenly aroused from a sound sleep. Here, as well as in spontaneous awakening, the first glance strikes the perception content created by the dream-work, while the next strikes the one produced from without.

But of greater theoretical interest are those dreams which are capable of waking us in the midst of sleep. We must bear in mind the expediency elsewhere universally demonstrated, and ask ourselves why the dream or the unconscious wish has the power to disturb sleep, *i.e.* the fulfillment of the foreconscious wish. This is probably due to certain relations of energy into which we have no insight. If we possessed such insight we should probably find that the freedom given to the dream and the expenditure of a certain amount of detached attention represent for the dream an economy in energy, keeping in view the fact that the unconscious must be held in check at night just as during the day. We know from experience that the dream, even if it interrupts sleep, repeatedly during the same night, still remains compatible with sleep. We wake up for an instant, and immediately resume our sleep. It is like driving off a fly during sleep, we awake *ad hoc*, and when we resume our sleep we have removed the disturbance. As demonstrated by familiar examples from the sleep of wet nurses, &c., the fulfillment of the wish to sleep is quite compatible with the retention of a certain amount of attention in a given direction.

But we must here take cognizance of an objection that is based on a better knowledge of the unconscious processes. Although we have ourselves described the unconscious wishes as always active, we have, nevertheless, asserted that they are not sufficiently strong during the day to make themselves perceptible. But when we sleep, and the unconscious wish has shown its power to form a dream, and with it to awaken the foreconscious, why, then, does this power become exhausted after the dream has been taken cognizance of? Would it not seem more probable that the dream should continually renew itself, like the troublesome fly which, when driven away, takes pleasure in returning again and again? What justifies our assertion that the dream removes the disturbance of sleep?

That the unconscious wishes always remain active is quite true. They represent paths which are passable whenever a sum of excitement makes use of them. Moreover, a remarkable peculiarity of the unconscious processes is the fact that they remain indestructible. Nothing can be brought to an end in the unconscious; nothing can

cease or be forgotten. This impression is most strongly gained in the study of the neuroses, especially of hysteria. The unconscious stream of thought which leads to the discharge through an attack becomes passable again as soon as there is an accumulation of a sufficient amount of excitement. The mortification brought on thirty years ago, after having gained access to the unconscious affective source, operates during all these thirty years like a recent one. Whenever its memory is touched, it is revived and shows itself to be supplied with the excitement which is discharged in a motor attack. It is just here that the office of psychotherapy begins, its task being to bring about adjustment and forgetfulness for the unconscious processes. Indeed, the fading of memories and the flagging of affects, which we are apt to take as self-evident and to explain as a primary influence of time on the psychic memories, are in reality secondary changes brought about by painstaking work. It is the foreconscious that accomplishes this work; and the only course to be pursued by psychotherapy is the subjugate the Unc, to the domination of the Forec.

There are, therefore, two exits for the individual unconscious emotional process. It is either left to itself, in which case it ultimately breaks through somewhere and secures for once a discharge for its excitation into motility; or it succumbs to the influence of the foreconscious, and its excitation becomes confined through this influence instead of being discharged. It is the latter process that occurs in the dream. Owing to the fact that it is directed by the conscious excitement, the energy from the Forec., which confronts the dream when grown to perception, restricts the unconscious excitement of the dream and renders it harmless as a disturbing factor. When the dreamer wakes up for a moment, he has actually chased away the fly that has threatened to disturb his sleep. We can now understand that it is really more expedient and economical to give full sway to the unconscious wish, and clear its way to regression so that it may form a dream, and then restrict and adjust this dream by means of a small expenditure of foreconscious labor, than to curb the unconscious throughout the entire period of sleep. We should, indeed, expect that the dream, even if it was not originally

an expedient process, would have acquired some function in the play of forces of the psychic life. We now see what this function is. The dream has taken it upon itself to bring the liberated excitement of the Unc. back under the domination of the foreconscious; it thus affords relief for the excitement of the Unc. and acts as a safety-valve for the latter, and at the same time it insures the sleep of the foreconscious at a slight expenditure of the waking state. Like the other psychic formations of its group, the dream offers itself as a compromise serving simultaneously both systems by fulfilling both wishes in so far as they are compatible with each other. A glance at Robert's "elimination theory," will show that we must agree with this author in his main point, viz. in the determination of the function of the dream, though we differ from him in our hypotheses and in our treatment of the dream process.

The above qualification–in so far as the two wishes are compatible with each other–contains a suggestion that there may be cases in which the function of the dream suffers shipwreck. The dream process is in the first instance admitted as a wish-fulfillment of the unconscious, but if this tentative wish-fulfillment disturbs the foreconscious to such an extent that the latter can no longer maintain its rest, the dream then breaks the compromise and fails to perform the second part of its task. It is then at once broken off, and replaced by complete wakefulness. Here, too, it is not really the fault of the dream, if, while ordinarily the guardian of sleep, it is here compelled to appear as the disturber of sleep, nor should this cause us to entertain any doubts as to its efficacy. This is not the only case in the organism in which an otherwise efficacious arrangement became inefficacious and disturbing as soon as some element is changed in the conditions of its origin; the disturbance then serves at least the new purpose of announcing the change, and calling into play against it the means of adjustment of the organism. In this connection, I naturally bear in mind the case of the anxiety dream, and in order not to have the appearance of trying to exclude this testimony against the theory of wish-fulfillment wherever I encounter it, I will attempt an explanation of the anxiety dream, at least offering some suggestions.

That a psychic process developing anxiety may still be a wish-fulfillment has long ceased to impress us as a contradiction. We may explain this occurrence by the fact that the wish belongs to one system (the Unc.), while by the other system (the Forec.), this wish has been rejected and suppressed. The subjection of the Unc. by the Forec. is not complete even in perfect psychic health; the amount of this suppression shows the degree of our psychic normality. Neurotic symptoms show that there is a conflict between the two systems; the symptoms are the results of a compromise of this conflict, and they temporarily put an end to it. On the one hand, they afford the Unc. an outlet for the discharge of its excitement, and serve it as a sally port, while, on the other hand, they give the Forec. the capability of dominating the Unc. to some extent. It is highly instructive to consider, *e.g.*, the significance of any hysterical phobia or of an agoraphobia. Suppose a neurotic incapable of crossing the street alone, which we would justly call a "symptom." We attempt to remove this symptom by urging him to the action which he deems himself incapable of. The result will be an attack of anxiety, just as an attack of anxiety in the street has often been the cause of establishing an agoraphobia. We thus learn that the symptom has been constituted in order to guard against the outbreak of the anxiety. The phobia is thrown before the anxiety like a fortress on the frontier.

Unless we enter into the part played by the affects in these processes, which can be done here only imperfectly, we cannot continue our discussion. Let us therefore advance the proposition that the reason why the suppression of the unconscious becomes absolutely necessary is because, if the discharge of presentation should be left to itself, it would develop an affect in the Unc. which originally bore the character of pleasure, but which, since the appearance of the repression, bears the character of pain. The aim, as well as the result, of the suppression is to stop the development of this pain. The suppression extends over the unconscious ideation, because the liberation of pain might emanate from the ideation. The foundation is here laid for a very definite assumption concerning the nature of the affective development. It is regarded as a motor or

secondary activity, the key to the innervation of which is located in the presentations of the Unc. Through the domination of the Forec. these presentations become, as it were, throttled and inhibited at the exit of the emotion-developing impulses. The danger, which is due to the fact that the Forec. ceases to occupy the energy, therefore consists in the fact that the unconscious excitations liberate such an affect as—in consequence of the repression that has previously taken place—can only be perceived as pain or anxiety.

This danger is released through the full sway of the dream process. The determinations for its realization consist in the fact that repressions have taken place, and that the suppressed emotional wishes shall become sufficiently strong. They thus stand entirely without the psychological realm of the dream structure. Were it not for the fact that our subject is connected through just one factor, namely, the freeing of the Unc. during sleep, with the subject of the development of anxiety, I could dispense with discussion of the anxiety dream, and thus avoid all obscurities connected with it.

As I have often repeated, the theory of the anxiety belongs to the psychology of the neuroses. I would say that the anxiety in the dream is an anxiety problem and not a dream problem. We have nothing further to do with it after having once demonstrated its point of contact with the subject of the dream process. There is only one thing left for me to do. As I have asserted that the neurotic anxiety originates from sexual sources, I can subject anxiety dreams to analysis in order to demonstrate the sexual material in their dream thoughts.

For good reasons I refrain from citing here any of the numerous examples placed at my disposal by neurotic patients, but prefer to give anxiety dreams from young persons.

Personally, I have had no real anxiety dream for decades, but I recall one from my seventh or eighth year which I subjected to interpretation about thirty years later. The dream was very vivid, and showed me *my beloved mother, with peculiarly calm sleeping countenance, carried into the room and laid on the bed by two (or three) persons with birds' beaks.* I awoke crying and screaming, and disturbed my parents. The very tall figures—draped

in a peculiar manner—with beaks, I had taken from the illustrations of Philippson's bible; I believe they represented deities with heads of sparrowhawks from an Egyptian tomb relief. The analysis also introduced the reminiscence of a naughty janitor's boy, who used to play with us children on the meadow in front of the house; I would add that his name was Philip. I feel that I first heard from this boy the vulgar word signifying sexual intercourse, which is replaced among the educated by the Latin "coitus," but to which the dream distinctly alludes by the selection of the birds' heads. I must have suspected the sexual significance of the word from the facial expression of my worldly-wise teacher. My mother's features in the dream were copied from the countenance of my grandfather, whom I had seen a few days before his death snoring in the state of coma. The interpretation of the secondary elaboration in the dream must therefore have been that my mother was dying; the tomb relief, too, agrees with this. In this anxiety I awoke, and could not calm myself until I had awakened my parents. I remember that I suddenly became calm on coming face to face with my mother, as if I needed the assurance that my mother was not dead. But this secondary interpretation of the dream had been effected only under the influence of the developed anxiety. I was not frightened because I dreamed that my mother was dying, but I interpreted the dream in this manner in the foreconscious elaboration because I was already under the domination of the anxiety. The latter, however, could be traced by means of the repression to an obscure obviously sexual desire, which had found its satisfying expression in the visual content of the dream.

A man twenty-seven years old who had been severely ill for a year had had many terrifying dreams between the ages of eleven and thirteen. He thought that a man with an ax was running after him; he wished to run, but felt paralyzed and could not move from the spot. This may be taken as a good example of a very common, and apparently sexually indifferent, anxiety dream. In the analysis the dreamer first thought of a story told him by his uncle, which chronologically was later than the dream, viz. that he was attacked at night by a suspicious-looking individual. This occurrence led him to believe that he himself might have already heard of a similar episode

at the time of the dream. In connection with the ax he recalled that during that period of his life he once hurt his hand with an ax while chopping wood. This immediately led to his relations with his younger brother, whom he used to maltreat and knock down. In particular, he recalled an occasion when he struck his brother on the head with his boot until he bled, whereupon his mother remarked: "I fear he will kill him some day." While he was seemingly thinking of the subject of violence, a reminiscence from his ninth year suddenly occurred to him. His parents came home late and went to bed while he was feigning sleep. He soon heard panting and other noises that appeared strange to him, and he could also make out the position of his parents in bed. His further associations showed that he had established an analogy between this relation between his parents and his own relation toward his younger brother. He subsumed what occurred between his parents under the conception "violence and wrestling," and thus reached a sadistic conception of the coitus act, as often happens among children. The fact that he often noticed blood on his mother's bed corroborated his conception.

That the sexual intercourse of adults appears strange to children who observe it, and arouses fear in them, I dare say is a fact of daily experience. I have explained this fear by the fact that sexual excitement is not mastered by their understanding, and is probably also inacceptable to them because their parents are involved in it. For the same son this excitement is converted into fear. At a still earlier period of life sexual emotion directed toward the parent of opposite sex does not meet with repression but finds free expression, as we have seen before.

For the night terrors with hallucinations (*pavor nocturnus*) frequently found in children, I would unhesitatingly give the same explanation. Here, too, we are certainly dealing with the incomprehensible and rejected sexual feelings, which, if noted, would probably show a temporal periodicity, for an enhancement of the sexual *libido* may just as well be produced accidentally through emotional impressions as through the spontaneous and gradual processes of development.

I lack the necessary material to sustain these explanations from observation. On the other hand, the pediatrists seem to lack the point of view which alone makes comprehensible the whole series of phenomena, on the somatic as well as on the psychic side. To illustrate by a comical example how one wearing the blinders of medical mythology may miss the understanding of such cases I will relate a case which I found in a thesis on *pavor nocturnus* by *Debacker*, 1881. A thirteen-year-old boy of delicate health began to become anxious and dreamy; his sleep became restless, and about once a week it was interrupted by an acute attack of anxiety with hallucinations. The memory of these dreams was invariably very distinct. Thus, he related that the *devil* shouted at him: "Now we have you, now we have you," and this was followed by an odor of sulphur; the fire burned his skin. This dream aroused him, terror-stricken. He was unable to scream at first; then his voice returned, and he was heard to say distinctly: "No, no, not me; why, I have done nothing," or, "Please don't, I shall never do it again." Occasionally, also, he said: "Albert has not done that." Later he avoided undressing, because, as he said, the fire attacked him only when he was undressed. From amid these evil dreams, which menaced his health, he was sent into the country, where he recovered within a year and a half, but at the age of fifteen he once confessed: "Je n'osais pas l'avouer, mais j'éprouvais continuellement des picotements et des surexcitations aux *parties*; à la fin, cela m'énervait tant que plusieurs fois, j'ai pensé me jeter par la fenêtre au dortoir."

It is certainly not difficult to suspect: 1, that the boy had practiced masturbation in former years, that he probably denied it, and was threatened with severe punishment for his wrongdoing (his confession: Je ne le ferai plus; his denial: Albert n'a jamais fait ça). 2, That under the pressure of puberty the temptation to self-abuse through the tickling of the genitals was reawakened. 3, That now, however, a struggle of repression arose in him, suppressing the *libido* and changing it into fear, which subsequently took the form of the punishments with which he was then threatened.

Let us, however, quote the conclusions drawn by our author. This observation shows:

1. That the influence of puberty may produce in a boy of delicate health a condition of extreme weakness, and that it may lead to a *very marked cerebral anæmia.*
2. This cerebral anæmia produces a transformation of character, demonomaniacal hallucinations, and very violent nocturnal, perhaps also diurnal, states of anxiety.
3. Demonomania and the self-reproaches of the day can be traced to the influences of religious education which the subject underwent as a child.
4. All manifestations disappeared as a result of a lengthy sojourn in the country, bodily exercise, and the return of physical strength after the termination of the period of puberty.
5. A predisposing influence for the origin of the cerebral condition of the boy may be attributed to heredity and to the father's chronic syphilitic state.

The concluding remarks of the author read: "Nous avons fait entrer cette observation dans le cadre des délires apyrétiques d'inanition, car c'est à l'ischémie cérébrale que nous rattachons cet état particulier."

◆◆◆

VIII

THE PRIMARY AND SECONDARY PROCESS—REGRESSION

In venturing to attempt to penetrate more deeply into the psychology of the dream processes, I have undertaken a difficult task, to which, indeed, my power of description is hardly equal. To reproduce in description by a succession of words the simultaneousness of so complex a chain of events, and in doing so to appear unbiassed throughout the exposition, goes fairly beyond my powers. I have now to atone for the fact that I have been unable in my description of the dream psychology to follow the historic development of my views. The view-points for my conception of the dream were reached through earlier investigations in the psychology of the neuroses, to which I am not supposed to refer here, but to which I am repeatedly forced to refer, whereas I should prefer to proceed in the opposite direction, and, starting from the dream, to establish a connection with the psychology of the neuroses. I am well aware of all the inconveniences arising for the reader from this difficulty, but I know of no way to avoid them.

As I am dissatisfied with this state of affairs, I am glad to dwell upon another view-point which seems to raise the value of my efforts. As has been shown in the introduction to the first chapter, I found myself confronted with a theme which had been marked by the sharpest contradictions on the part of the authorities. After our elaboration of the dream problems we found room for most of these contradictions. We have been forced, however, to take decided

exception to two of the views pronounced, viz. that the dream is a senseless and that it is a somatic process; apart from these cases we have had to accept all the contradictory views in one place or another of the complicated argument, and we have been able to demonstrate that they had discovered something that was correct. That the dream continues the impulses and interests of the waking state has been quite generally confirmed through the discovery of the latent thoughts of the dream. These thoughts concern themselves only with things that seem important and of momentous interest to us. The dream never occupies itself with trifles. But we have also concurred with the contrary view, viz., that the dream gathers up the indifferent remnants from the day, and that not until it has in some measure withdrawn itself from the waking activity can an important event of the day be taken up by the dream. We found this holding true for the dream content, which gives the dream thought its changed expression by means of disfigurement. We have said that from the nature of the association mechanism the dream process more easily takes possession of recent or indifferent material which has not yet been seized by the waking mental activity; and by reason of the censor it transfers the psychic intensity from the important but also disagreeable to the indifferent material. The hypermnesia of the dream and the resort to infantile material have become main supports in our theory. In our theory of the dream we have attributed to the wish originating from the infantile the part of an indispensable motor for the formation of the dream. We naturally could not think of doubting the experimentally demonstrated significance of the objective sensory stimuli during sleep; but we have brought this material into the same relation to the dream-wish as the thought remnants from the waking activity. There was no need of disputing the fact that the dream interprets the objective sensory stimuli after the manner of an illusion; but we have supplied the motive for this interpretation which has been left undecided by the authorities. The interpretation follows in such a manner that the perceived object is rendered harmless as a sleep disturber and becomes available for the wish-fulfillment. Though we do not admit as special sources of the dream the subjective state

of excitement of the sensory organs during sleep, which seems to have been demonstrated by Trumbull Ladd, we are nevertheless able to explain this excitement through the regressive revival of active memories behind the dream. A modest part in our conception has also been assigned to the inner organic sensations which are wont to be taken as the cardinal point in the explanation of the dream. These–the sensation of falling, flying, or inhibition–stand as an ever ready material to be used by the dream-work to express the dream thought as often as need arises.

That the dream process is a rapid and momentary one seems to be true for the perception through consciousness of the already prepared dream content; the preceding parts of the dream process probably take a slow, fluctuating course. We have solved the riddle of the superabundant dream content compressed within the briefest moment by explaining that this is due to the appropriation of almost fully formed structures from the psychic life. That the dream is disfigured and distorted by memory we found to be correct, but not troublesome, as this is only the last manifest operation in the work of disfigurement which has been active from the beginning of the dream-work. In the bitter and seemingly irreconcilable controversy as to whether the psychic life sleeps at night or can make the same use of all its capabilities as during the day, we have been able to agree with both sides, though not fully with either. We have found proof that the dream thoughts represent a most complicated intellectual activity, employing almost every means furnished by the psychic apparatus; still it cannot be denied that these dream thoughts have originated during the day, and it is indispensable to assume that there is a sleeping state of the psychic life. Thus, even the theory of partial sleep has come into play; but the characteristics of the sleeping state have been found not in the dilapidation of the psychic connections but in the cessation of the psychic system dominating the day, arising from its desire to sleep. The withdrawal from the outer world retains its significance also for our conception; though not the only factor, it nevertheless helps the regression to make possible the representation of the dream. That we should reject the voluntary

guidance of the presentation course is uncontestable; but the psychic life does not thereby become aimless, for we have seen that after the abandonment of the desired end-presentation undesired ones gain the mastery. The loose associative connection in the dream we have not only recognized, but we have placed under its control a far greater territory than could have been supposed; we have, however, found it merely the feigned substitute for another correct and senseful one. To be sure we, too, have called the dream absurd; but we have been able to learn from examples how wise the dream really is when it simulates absurdity. We do not deny any of the functions that have been attributed to the dream. That the dream relieves the mind like a valve, and that, according to Robert's assertion, all kinds of harmful material are rendered harmless through representation in the dream, not only exactly coincides with our theory of the twofold wish-fulfillment in the dream, but, in his own wording, becomes even more comprehensible for us than for Robert himself. The free indulgence of the psychic in the play of its faculties finds expression with us in the non-interference with the dream on the part of the foreconscious activity. The "return to the embryonal state of psychic life in the dream" and the observation of Havelock Ellis, "an archaic world of vast emotions and imperfect thoughts," appear to us as happy anticipations of our deductions to the effect that *primitive* modes of work suppressed during the day participate in the formation of the dream; and with us, as with Delage, the *suppressed* material becomes the mainspring of the dreaming.

We have fully recognized the rôle which Scherner ascribes to the dream phantasy, and even his interpretation; but we have been obliged, so to speak, to conduct them to another department in the problem. It is not the dream that produces the phantasy but the unconscious phantasy that takes the greatest part in the formation of the dream thoughts. We are indebted to Scherner for his clew to the source of the dream thoughts, but almost everything that he ascribes to the dream-work is attributable to the activity of the unconscious, which is at work during the day, and which supplies incitements not only for dreams

but for neurotic symptoms as well. We have had to separate the dream-work from this activity as being something entirely different and far more restricted. Finally, we have by no means abandoned the relation of the dream to mental disturbances, but, on the contrary, we have given it a more solid foundation on new ground.

Thus held together by the new material of our theory as by a superior unity, we find the most varied and most contradictory conclusions of the authorities fitting into our structure; some of them are differently disposed, only a few of them are entirely rejected. But our own structure is still unfinished. For, disregarding the many obscurities which we have necessarily encountered in our advance into the darkness of psychology, we are now apparently embarrassed by a new contradiction. On the one hand, we have allowed the dream thoughts to proceed from perfectly normal mental operations, while, on the other hand, we have found among the dream thoughts a number of entirely abnormal mental processes which extend likewise to the dream contents. These, consequently, we have repeated in the interpretation of the dream. All that we have termed the "dream-work" seems so remote from the psychic processes recognized by us as correct, that the severest judgments of the authors as to the low psychic activity of dreaming seem to us well founded.

Perhaps only through still further advance can enlightenment and improvement be brought about. I shall pick out one of the constellations leading to the formation of dreams.

We have learned that the dream replaces a number of thoughts derived from daily life which are perfectly formed logically. We cannot therefore doubt that these thoughts originate from our normal mental life. All the qualities which we esteem in our mental operations, and which distinguish these as complicated activities of a high order, we find repeated in the dream thoughts. There is, however, no need of assuming that this mental work is performed during sleep, as this would materially impair the conception of the psychic state of sleep we have hitherto adhered to. These thoughts may just as well have originated from the day, and, unnoticed by our consciousness

from their inception, they may have continued to develop until they stood complete at the onset of sleep. If we are to conclude anything from this state of affairs, it will at most prove *that the most complex mental operations are possible without the coöperation of consciousness*, which wc have already learned independently from every psychoanalysis of persons suffering from hysteria or obsessions. These dream thoughts are in themselves surely not incapable of consciousness; if they have not become conscious to us during the day, this may have various reasons. The state of becoming conscious depends on the exercise of a certain psychic function, viz. attention, which seems to be extended only in a definite quantity, and which may have been withdrawn from the stream of thought in Question by other aims. Another way in which such mental streams are kept from consciousness is the following:–Our conscious reflection teaches us that when exercising attention we pursue a definite course. But if that course leads us to an idea which does not hold its own with the critic, we discontinue and cease to apply our attention. Now, apparently, the stream of thought thus started and abandoned may spin on without regaining attention unless it reaches a spot of especially marked intensity which forces the return of attention. An initial rejection, perhaps consciously brought about by the judgment on the ground of incorrectness or unfitness for the actual purpose of the mental act, may therefore account for the fact that a mental process continues until the onset of sleep unnoticed by consciousness.

Let us recapitulate by saying that we call such a stream of thought a foreconscious one, that we believe it to be perfectly correct, and that it may just as well be a more neglected one or an interrupted and suppressed one. Let us also state frankly in what manner we conceive this presentation course. We believe that a certain sum of excitement, which we call occupation energy, is displaced from an end-presentation along the association paths selected by that end-presentation. A "neglected" stream of thought has received no such occupation, and from a "suppressed" or "rejected" one this occupation has been withdrawn; both have thus been left to their own emotions.

The end-stream of thought stocked with energy is under certain conditions able to draw to itself the attention of consciousness, through which means it then receives a "surplus of energy." We shall be obliged somewhat later to elucidate our assumption concerning the nature and activity of consciousness.

A train of thought thus incited in the Forec. may either disappear spontaneously or continue. The former issue we conceive as follows: It diffuses its energy through all the association paths emanating from it, and throws the entire chain of ideas into a state of excitement which, after lasting for a while, subsides through the transformation of the excitement requiring an outlet into dormant energy.[23] If this first issue is brought about the process has no further significance for the dream formation. But other end-presentations are lurking in our foreconscious that originate from the sources of our unconscious and from the ever active wishes. These may take possession of the excitations in the circle of thought thus left to itself, establish a connection between it and the unconscious wish, and transfer to it the energy inherent in the unconscious wish. Henceforth the neglected or suppressed train of thought is in a position to maintain itself, although this reinforcement does not help it to gain access to consciousness. We may say that the hitherto foreconscious train of thought has been drawn into the unconscious.

Other constellations for the dream formation would result if the foreconscious train of thought had from the beginning been connected with the unconscious wish, and for that reason met with rejection by the dominating end-occupation; or if an unconscious wish were made active for other—possibly somatic—reasons and of its own accord sought a transference to the psychic remnants not occupied by the Forec. All three cases finally combine in one issue, so that there is established in the foreconscious a stream of thought which, having been abandoned by the foreconscious occupation, receives occupation from the unconscious wish.

The stream of thought is henceforth subjected to a series of

---

23. *Cf.* the significant observations by J. Bueuer in our *Studies on Hysteria*, 1895, and 2nd ed. 1909.

transformations which we no longer recognize as normal psychic processes and which give us a surprising result, viz. a psychopathological formation. Let us emphasize and group the same.

1. The intensities of the individual ideas become capable of discharge in their entirety, and, proceeding from one conception to the other, they thus form single presentations endowed with marked intensity. Through the repeated recurrence of this process the intensity of an entire train of ideas may ultimately be gathered in a single presentation element. This is the principle of *compression or condensation.* It is condensation that is mainly responsible for the strange impression of the dream, for we know of nothing analogous to it in the normal psychic life accessible to consciousness. We find here, also, presentations which possess great psychic significance as junctions or as end-results of whole chains of thought; but this validity does not manifest itself in any character conspicuous enough for internal perception; hence, what has been presented in it does not become in any way more intensive. In the process of condensation the entire psychic connection becomes transformed into the intensity of the presentation content. It is the same as in a book where we space or print in heavy type any word upon which particular stress is laid for the understanding of the text. In speech the same word would be pronounced loudly and deliberately and with emphasis. The first comparison leads us at once to an example taken from the chapter on "The Dream-Work" (trimethylamine in the dream of Irma's injection). Historians of art call our attention to the fact that the most ancient historical sculptures follow a similar principle in expressing the rank of the persons represented by the size of the statue. The king is made two or three times as large as his retinue or the vanquished enemy. A piece of art, however, from the Roman period makes use of more subtle means to accomplish the same purpose. The figure of the emperor is placed in

the center in a firmly erect posture; special care is bestowed on the proper modelling of his figure; his enemies are seen cowering at his feet; but he is no longer represented a giant among dwarfs. However, the bowing of the subordinate to his superior in our own days is only an echo of that ancient principle of representation.

The direction taken by the condensations of the dream is prescribed on the one hand by the true foreconscious relations of the dream thoughts, an the other hand by the attraction of the visual reminiscences in the unconscious. The success of the condensation work produces those intensities which are required for penetration into the perception systems.

1. Through this free transferability of the intensities, moreover, and in the service of condensation, *intermediary presentations*—compromises, as it were—are formed (*cf.* the numerous examples). This, likewise, is something unheard of in the normal presentation course, where it is above all a question of selection and retention of the "proper" presentation element. On the other hand, composite and compromise formations occur with extraordinary frequency when we are trying to find the linguistic expression for foreconscious thoughts; these are considered "slips of the tongue."

2. The presentations which transfer their intensities to one another are *very loosely connected*, and are joined together by such forms of association as are spurned in our serious thought and are utilized in the production of the effect of wit only. Among these we particularly find associations of the sound and consonance types.

3. Contradictory thoughts do not strive to eliminate one another, but remain side by side. They often unite to produce condensation *as if no contradiction* existed, or they form compromises for which we should never forgive our thoughts, but which we frequently approve of in our actions.

These are some of the most conspicuous abnormal processes to which the thoughts which have previously been rationally formed are subjected in the course of the dream-work. As the main feature of these processes we recognize the high importance attached to the fact of rendering the occupation energy mobile and capable of discharge; the content and the actual significance of the psychic elements, to which these energies adhere, become a matter of secondary importance. One might possibly think that the condensation and compromise formation is effected only in the service of regression, when occasion arises for changing thoughts into pictures. But the analysis and—still more distinctly—the synthesis of dreams which lack regression toward pictures, *e.g.* the dream "Autodidasker—Conversation with Court-Councilor N.," present the same processes of displacement and condensation as the others.

Hence we cannot refuse to acknowledge that the two kinds of essentially different psychic processes participate in the formation of the dream; one forms perfectly correct dream thoughts which are equivalent to normal thoughts, while the other treats these ideas in a highly surprising and incorrect manner. The latter process we have already set apart as the dream-work proper. What have we now to advance concerning this latter psychic process?

We should be unable to answer this question here if we had not penetrated considerably into the psychology of the neuroses and especially of hysteria. From this we learn that the same incorrect psychic processes—as well as others that have not been enumerated—control the formation of hysterical symptoms. In hysteria, too, we at once find a series of perfectly correct thoughts equivalent to our conscious thoughts, of whose existence, however, in this form we can learn nothing and which we can only subsequently reconstruct. If they have forced their way anywhere to our perception, we discover from the analysis of the symptom formed that these normal thoughts have been subjected to abnormal treatment and *have been transformed into the symptom by means of condensation and compromise formation, through*

superficial associations, under cover of contradictions, and eventually over the road of regression. In view of the complete identity found between the peculiarities of the dream-work and of the psychic activity forming the psychoneurotic symptoms, we shall feel justified in transferring to the dream the conclusions urged upon us by hysteria.

From the theory of hysteria we borrow the proposition that *such an abnormal psychic elaboration of a normal train of thought takes place only when the latter has been used for the transference of an unconscious wish which dates from the infantile life and is in a state of repression.* In accordance with this proposition we have construed the theory of the dream on the assumption that the actuating dream-wish invariably originates in the unconscious, which, as we ourselves have admitted, cannot be universally demonstrated though it cannot be refuted. But in order to explain the real meaning of the term *repression*, which we have employed so freely, we shall be obliged to make some further addition to our psychological construction.

We have above elaborated the fiction of a primitive psychic apparatus, whose work is regulated by the efforts to avoid accumulation of excitement and as far as possible to maintain itself free from excitement. For this reason it was constructed after the plan of a reflex apparatus; the motility, originally the path for the inner bodily change, formed a discharging path standing at its disposal. We subsequently discussed the psychic results of a feeling of gratification, and we might at the same time have introduced the second assumption, viz. that accumulation of excitement–following certain modalities that do not concern us–is perceived as pain and sets the apparatus in motion in order to reproduce a feeling of gratification in which the diminution of the excitement is perceived as pleasure. Such a current in the apparatus which emanates from pain and strives for pleasure we call a wish. We have said that nothing but a wish is capable of setting the apparatus in motion, and that the discharge of excitement in the apparatus is regulated automatically by the perception of pleasure and pain. The first wish must have been an hallucinatory occupation of the memory for gratification. But this

hallucination, unless it were maintained to the point of exhaustion, proved incapable of bringing about a cessation of the desire and consequently of securing the pleasure connected with gratification.

Thus there was required a second activity—in our terminology the activity of a second system—which should not permit the memory occupation to advance to perception and therefrom to restrict the psychic forces, but should lead the excitement emanating from the craving stimulus by a devious path over the spontaneous motility which ultimately should so change the outer world as to allow the real perception of the object of gratification to take place. Thus far we have elaborated the plan of the psychic apparatus; these two systems are the germ of the Unc. and Forec, which we include in the fully developed apparatus.

In order to be in a position successfully to change the outer world through the motility, there is required the accumulation of a large sum of experiences in the memory systems as well as a manifold fixation of the relations which are evoked in this memory material by different end-presentations. We now proceed further with our assumption. The manifold activity of the second system, tentatively sending forth and retracting energy, must on the one hand have full command over all memory material, but on the other hand it would be a superfluous expenditure for it to send to the individual mental paths large quantities of energy which would thus flow off to no purpose, diminishing the quantity available for the transformation of the outer world. In the interests of expediency I therefore postulate that the second system succeeds in maintaining the greater part of the occupation energy in a dormant state and in using but a small portion for the purposes of displacement. The mechanism of these processes is entirely unknown to me; any one who wishes to follow up these ideas must try to find the physical analogies and prepare the way for a demonstration of the process of motion in the stimulation of the neuron. I merely hold to the idea that the activity of the first Ψ-system is directed *to the free outflow of*

the quantities of excitement, and that the second system brings about an inhibition of this outflow through the energies emanating from it, *i.e.* it produces a *transformation into dormant energy, probably by raising the level.* I therefore assume that under the control of the second system as compared with the first, the course of the excitement is bound to entirely different mechanical conditions. After the second system has finished its tentative mental work, it removes the inhibition and congestion of the excitements and allows these excitements to flow off to the motility.

An interesting train of thought now presents itself if we consider the relations of this inhibition of discharge by the second system to the regulation through the principle of pain. Let us now seek the counterpart of the primary feeling of gratification, namely, the objective feeling of fear. A perceptive stimulus acts on the primitive apparatus, becoming the source of a painful emotion. This will then be followed by irregular motor manifestations until one of these withdraws the apparatus from perception and at the same time from pain, but on the reappearance of the perception this manifestation will immediately repeat itself (perhaps as a movement of flight) until the perception has again disappeared. But there will here remain no tendency again to occupy the perception of the source of pain in the form of an hallucination or in any other form. On the contrary, there will be a tendency in the primary apparatus to abandon the painful memory picture as soon as it is in any way awakened, as the overflow of its excitement would surely produce (more precisely, begin to produce) pain. The deviation from memory, which is but a repetition of the former flight from perception, is facilitated also by the fact that, unlike perception, memory does not possess sufficient quality to excite consciousness and thereby to attract to itself new energy. This easy and regularly occurring deviation of the psychic process from the former painful memory presents to us the model and the first example of *psychic repression.* As is generally known, much of this deviation from the painful, much of the behavior of the ostrich, can be readily demonstrated even in the normal psychic life of adults.

By virtue of the principle of pain the first system is therefore altogether incapable of introducing anything unpleasant into the mental associations. The system cannot do anything but wish. If this remained so the mental activity of the second system, which should have at its disposal all the memories stored up by experiences, would be hindered. But two ways are now opened: the work of the second system either frees itself completely from the principle of pain and continues its course, paying no heed to the painful reminiscence, or it contrives to occupy the painful memory in such a manner as to preclude the liberation of pain. We may reject the first possibility, as the principle of pain also manifests itself as a regulator for the emotional discharge of the second system; we are, therefore, directed to the second possibility, namely, that this system occupies a reminiscence in such a manner as to inhibit its discharge and hence, also, to inhibit the discharge comparable to a motor innervation for the development of pain. Thus from two starting points we are led to the hypothesis that occupation through the second system is at the same time an inhibition for the emotional discharge, viz. from a consideration of the principle of pain and from the principle of the smallest expenditure of innervation. Let us, however, keep to the fact–this is the key to the theory of repression–that the second system is capable of occupying an idea only when it is in position to check the development of pain emanating from it. Whatever withdraws itself from this inhibition also remains inaccessible for the second system and would soon be abandoned by virtue of the principle of pain. The inhibition of pain, however, need not be complete; it must be permitted to begin, as it indicates to the second system the nature of the memory and possibly its defective adaptation for the purpose sought by the mind.

The psychic process which is admitted by the first system only I shall now call the *primary* process; and the one resulting from the inhibition of the second system I shall call the *secondary* process. I show by another point for what purpose the second system is obliged to correct the primary process. The primary process strives for a discharge

of the excitement in order to establish a *perception* identity with the sum of excitement thus gathered; the secondary process has abandoned this intention and undertaken instead the task of bringing about a *thought identity*. All thinking is only a circuitous path from the memory of gratification taken as an end-presentation to the identical occupation of the same memory, which is again to be attained on the track of the motor experiences. The state of thinking must take an interest in the connecting paths between the presentations without allowing itself to be misled by their intensities. But it is obvious that condensations and intermediate or compromise formations occurring in the presentations impede the attainment of this end-identity; by substituting one idea for the other they deviate from the path which otherwise would have been continued from the original idea. Such processes are therefore carefully avoided in the secondary thinking. Nor is it difficult to understand that the principle of pain also impedes the progress of the mental stream in its pursuit of the thought identity, though, indeed, it offers to the mental stream the most important points of departure. Hence the tendency of the thinking process must be to free itself more and more from exclusive adjustment by the principle of pain, and through the working of the mind to restrict the affective development to that minimum which is necessary as a signal. This refinement of the activity must have been attained through a recent over-occupation of energy brought about by consciousness. But we are aware that this refinement is seldom completely successful even in the most normal psychic life and that our thoughts ever remain accessible to falsification through the interference of the principle of pain.

This, however, is not the breach in the functional efficiency of our psychic apparatus through which the thoughts forming the material of the secondary mental work are enabled to make their way into the primary psychic process—with which formula we may now describe the work leading to the dream and to the hysterical symptoms. This case of insufficiency results from the union of the two factors from the history of our evolution; one of which belongs solely to the psychic

apparatus and has exerted a determining influence on the relation of the two systems, while the other operates fluctuatingly and introduces motive forces of organic origin into the psychic life. Both originate in the infantile life and result from the transformation which our psychic and somatic organism has undergone since the infantile period.

When I termed one of the psychic processes in the psychic apparatus the primary process, I did so not only in consideration of the order of precedence and capability, but also as admitting the temporal relations to a share in the nomenclature. As far as our knowledge goes there is no psychic apparatus possessing only the primary process, and in so far it is a theoretic fiction; but so much is based on fact that the primary processes are present in the apparatus from the beginning, while the secondary processes develop gradually in the course of life, inhibiting and covering the primary ones, and gaining complete mastery over them perhaps only at the height of life. Owing to this retarded appearance of the secondary processes, the essence of our being, consisting in unconscious wish feelings, can neither be seized nor inhibited by the foreconscious, whose part is once for all restricted to the indication of the most suitable paths for the wish feelings originating in the unconscious. These unconscious wishes establish for all subsequent psychic efforts a compulsion to which they have to submit and which they must strive if possible to divert from its course and direct to higher aims. In consequence of this retardation of the foreconscious occupation a large sphere of the memory material remains inaccessible.

Among these indestructible and unincumbered wish feelings originating from the infantile life, there are also some, the fulfillments of which have entered into a relation of contradiction to the end-presentation of the secondary thinking. The fulfillment of these wishes would no longer produce an affect of pleasure but one of pain; *and it is just this transformation of affect that constitutes the nature of what we designate as "repression," in which we recognize the infantile first step of passing adverse sentence or of rejecting through reason.* To investigate in what

way and through what motive forces such a transformation can be produced constitutes the problem of repression, which we need here only skim over. It will suffice to remark that such a transformation of affect occurs in the course of development (one may think of the appearance in infantile life of disgust which was originally absent), and that it is connected with the activity of the secondary system. The memories from which the unconscious wish brings about the emotional discharge have never been accessible to the Forec., and for that reason their emotional discharge cannot be inhibited. It is just on account of this affective development that these ideas are not even now accessible to the foreconscious thoughts to which they have transferred their wishing power. On the contrary, the principle of pain comes into play, and causes the Forec. to deviate from these thoughts of transference. The latter, left to themselves, are "repressed," and thus the existence of a store of infantile memories, from the very beginning withdrawn from the Forec., becomes the preliminary condition of repression.

In the most favorable case the development of pain terminates as soon as the energy has been withdrawn from the thoughts of transference in the Forec., and this effect characterizes the intervention of the principle of pain as expedient. It is different, however, if the repressed unconscious wish receives an organic enforcement which it can lend to its thoughts of transference and through which it can enable them to make an effort towards penetration with their excitement, even after they have been abandoned by the occupation of the Forec. A defensive struggle then ensues, inasmuch as the Forec. reinforces the antagonism against the repressed ideas, and subsequently this leads to a penetration by the thoughts of transference (the carriers of the unconscious wish) in some form of compromise through symptom formation. But from the moment that the suppressed thoughts are powerfully occupied by the unconscious wish-feeling and abandoned by the foreconscious occupation, they succumb to the primary psychic process and strive only for motor discharge; or, if the path

be free, for hallucinatory revival of the desired perception identity. We have previously found, empirically, that the incorrect processes described are enacted only with thoughts that exist in the repression. We now grasp another part of the connection. These incorrect processes are those that are primary in the psychic apparatus; *they appear wherever thoughts abandoned by the foreconscious occupation are left to themselves, and can fill themselves with the uninhibited energy, striving for discharge from the unconscious.* We may add a few further observations to support the view that these processes designated "incorrect" are really not falsifications of the normal defective thinking, but the modes of activity of the psychic apparatus when freed from inhibition. Thus we see that the transference of the foreconscious excitement to the motility takes place according to the same processes, and that the connection of the foreconscious presentations with words readily manifest the same displacements and mixtures which are ascribed to inattention. Finally, I should like to adduce proof that an increase of work necessarily results from the inhibition of these primary courses from the fact that we gain a *comical effect*, a surplus to be discharged through laughter, *if we allow these streams of thought to come to consciousness.*

The theory of the psychoneuroses asserts with complete certainty that only sexual wish-feelings from the infantile life experience repression (emotional transformation) during the developmental period of childhood. These are capable of returning to activity at a later period of development, and then have the faculty of being revived, either as a consequence of the sexual constitution, which is really formed from the original bisexuality, or in consequence of unfavorable influences of the sexual life; and they thus supply the motive power for all psychoneurotic symptom formations. It is only by the introduction of these sexual forces that the gaps still demonstrable in the theory of repression can be filled. I will leave it undecided whether the postulate of the sexual and infantile may also be asserted for the theory of the dream; I leave this here unfinished because I have already passed a step beyond the demonstrable in assuming that the dream-wish invariably

originates from the unconscious.[24] Nor will I further investigate the difference in the play of the psychic forces in the dream formation and in the formation of the hysterical symptoms, for to do this we ought to possess a more explicit knowledge of one of the members to be compared. But I regard another point as important, and will here confess that it was on account of this very point that I have just undertaken this entire discussion concerning the two psychic systems, their modes of operation, and the repression. For it is now immaterial whether I have conceived the psychological relations in question with approximate correctness, or, as is easily possible in such a difficult matter, in an erroneous and fragmentary manner. Whatever changes may be made in the interpretation of the psychic censor and of the correct and of the abnormal elaboration of the

---

24. Here, as in other places, there are gaps in the treatment of the subject, which I have left intentionally, because to fill them up would require on the one hand too great effort, and on the other hand an extensive reference to material that is foreign to the dream. Thus I have avoided stating whether I connect with the word "suppressed" another sense than with the word "repressed." It has been made clear only that the latter emphasizes more than the former the relation to the unconscious. I have not entered into the cognate problem why the dream thoughts also experience distortion by the censor when they abandon the progressive continuation to consciousness and choose the path of regression. I have been above all anxious to awaken an interest in the problems to which the further analysis of the dreamwork leads and to indicate the other themes which meet these on the way. It was not always easy to decide just where the pursuit should be discontinued. That I have not treated exhaustively the part played in the dream by the psychosexual life and have avoided the interpretation of dreams of an obvious sexual content is due to a special reason which may not come up to the reader's expectation. To be sure, it is very far from my ideas and the principles expressed by me in neuropathology to regard the sexual life as a "pudendum" which should be left unconsidered by the physician and the scientific investigator. I also consider ludicrous the moral indignation which prompted the translator of Artemidoros of Daldis to keep from the reader's knowledge the chapter on sexual dreams contained in the *Symbolism of the Dreams*. As for myself, I have been actuated solely by the conviction that in the explanation of sexual dreams I should be bound to entangle myself deeply in the still unexplained problems of perversion and bisexuality; and for that reason I have reserved this material for another connection.

dream content, the fact nevertheless remains that such processes are active in dream formation, and that essentially they show the closest analogy to the processes observed in the formation of the hysterical symptoms. The dream is not a pathological phenomenon, and it does not leave behind an enfeeblement of the mental faculties. The objection that no deduction can be drawn regarding the dreams of healthy persons from my own dreams and from those of neurotic patients may be rejected without comment. Hence, when we draw conclusions from the phenomena as to their motive forces, we recognize that the psychic mechanism made use of by the neuroses is not created by a morbid disturbance of the psychic life, but is found ready in the normal structure of the psychic apparatus. The two psychic systems, the censor crossing between them, the inhibition and the covering of the one activity by the other, the relations of both to consciousness—or whatever may offer a more correct interpretation of the actual conditions in their stead—all these belong to the normal structure of our psychic instrument, and the dream points out for us one of the roads leading to a knowledge of this structure. If, in addition to our knowledge, we wish to be contented with a minimum perfectly established, we shall say that the dream gives us proof that the *suppressed, material continues to exist even in the normal person and remains capable of psychic activity*. The dream itself is one of the manifestations of this suppressed material; theoretically, this is true in *all* cases; according to substantial experience it is true in at least a great number of such as most conspicuously display the prominent characteristics of dream life. The suppressed psychic material, which in the waking state has been prevented from expression and cut off from internal perception *by the antagonistic adjustment of the contradictions*, finds ways and means of obtruding itself on consciousness during the night under the domination of the compromise formations.

"Flectere si nequeo superos, Acheronta movebo."

At any rate the interpretation of dreams is the *via regia* to a knowledge of the unconscious in the psychic life.

In following the analysis of the dream we have made some progress toward an understanding of the composition of this most marvelous and most mysterious of instruments; to be sure, we have not gone very far, but enough of a beginning has been made to allow us to advance from other so-called pathological formations further into the analysis of the unconscious. Disease—at least that which is justly termed functional—is not due to the destruction of this apparatus, and the establishment of new splittings in its interior; it is rather to be explained dynamically through the strengthening and weakening of the components in the play of forces by which so many activities are concealed during the normal function. We have been able to show in another place how the composition of the apparatus from the two systems permits a subtilization even of the normal activity which would be impossible for a single system.

◆◆◆

IX

THE UNCONSCIOUS AND CONSCIOUSNESS—REALITY

On closer inspection we find that it is not the existence of two systems near the motor end of the apparatus but of two kinds of processes or modes of emotional discharge, the assumption of which was explained in the psychological discussions of the previous chapter. This can make no difference for us, for we must always be ready to drop our auxiliary ideas whenever we deem ourselves in position to replace them by something else approaching more closely to the unknown reality. Let us now try to correct some views which might be erroneously formed as long as we regarded the two systems in the crudest and most obvious sense as two localities within the psychic apparatus, views which have left their traces in the terms "repression" and "penetration." Thus, when we say that an unconscious idea strives for transference into the foreconscious in order later to penetrate consciousness, we do not mean that a second idea is to be formed situated in a new locality like an interlineation near which the original continues to remain; also, when we speak of penetration into consciousness, we wish carefully to avoid any idea of change of locality. When we say that a foreconscious idea is repressed and subsequently taken up by the unconscious, we might be tempted by these figures, borrowed from the idea of a struggle over a territory, to assume that an arrangement is really broken up in one psychic locality and replaced by a new one in the other locality. For these

comparisons we substitute what would seem to correspond better with the real state of affairs by saying that an energy occupation is displaced to or withdrawn from a certain arrangement so that the psychic formation falls under the domination of a system or is withdrawn from the same. Here again we replace a topical mode of presentation by a dynamic; it is not the psychic formation that appears to us as the moving factor but the innervation of the same.

I deem it appropriate and justifiable, however, to apply ourselves still further to the illustrative conception of the two systems. We shall avoid any misapplication of this manner of representation if we remember that presentations, thoughts, and psychic formations should generally not be localized in the organic elements of the nervous system, but, so to speak, between them, where resistances and paths form the correlate corresponding to them. Everything that can become an object of our internal perception is virtual, like the image in the telescope produced by the passage of the rays of light. But we are justified in assuming the existence of the systems, which have nothing psychic in themselves and which never become accessible to our psychic perception, corresponding to the lenses of the telescope which design the image. If we continue this comparison, we may say that the censor between two systems corresponds to the refraction of rays during their passage into a new medium.

Thus far we have made psychology on our own responsibility; it is now time to examine the theoretical opinions governing present-day psychology and to test their relation to our theories. The question of the unconscious, in psychology is, according to the authoritative words of Lipps, less a psychological question than the question of psychology. As long as psychology settled this question with the verbal explanation that the "psychic" is the "conscious" and that "unconscious psychic occurrences" are an obvious contradiction, a psychological estimate of the observations gained by the physician from abnormal mental states was precluded. The physician and the philosopher agree only when both acknowledge that unconscious psychic processes are "the appropriate and well-justified expression for an established fact." The

physician cannot but reject with a shrug of his shoulders the assertion that "consciousness is the indispensable quality of the psychic"; he may assume, if his respect for the utterings of the philosophers still be strong enough, that he and they do not treat the same subject and do not pursue the same science. For a single intelligent observation of the psychic life of a neurotic, a single analysis of a dream must force upon him the unalterable conviction that the most complicated and correct mental operations, to which no one will refuse the name of psychic occurrences, may take place without exciting the consciousness of the person. It is true that the physician does not learn of these unconscious processes until they have exerted such an effect on consciousness as to admit communication or observation. But this effect of consciousness may show a psychic character widely differing from the unconscious process, so that the internal perception cannot possibly recognize the one as a substitute for the other. The physician must reserve for himself the right to penetrate, by a process of deduction, from the effect on consciousness to the unconscious psychic process; he learns in this way that the effect on consciousness is only a remote psychic product of the unconscious process and that the latter has not become conscious as such; that it has been in existence and operative without betraying itself in any way to consciousness.

A reaction from the over-estimation of the quality of consciousness becomes the indispensable preliminary condition for any correct insight into the behavior of the psychic. In the words of Lipps, the unconscious must be accepted as the general basis of the psychic life. The unconscious is the larger circle which includes within itself the smaller circle of the conscious; everything conscious has its preliminary step in the unconscious, whereas the unconscious may stop with this step and still claim full value as a psychic activity. Properly speaking, the unconscious is the real psychic; *its inner nature is just as unknown to us as the reality of the external world, and it is just as imperfectly reported to us through the data of consciousness as is the external world through the indications of our sensory organs.*

A series of dream problems which have intensely occupied older authors will be laid aside when the old opposition between conscious life and dream life is abandoned and the unconscious psychic assigned to its proper place. Thus many of the activities whose performances in the dream have excited our admiration are now no longer to be attributed to the dream but to unconscious thinking, which is also active during the day. If, according to Scherner, the dream seems to play with a symboling representation of the body, we know that this is the work of certain unconscious phantasies which have probably given in to sexual emotions, and that these phantasies come to expression not only in dreams but also in hysterical phobias and in other symptoms. If the dream continues and settles activities of the day and even brings to light valuable inspirations, we have only to subtract from it the dream disguise as a feat of dream-work and a mark of assistance from obscure forces in the depth of the mind (*cf.* the devil in Tartini's sonata dream). The intellectual task as such must be attributed to the same psychic forces which perform all such tasks during the day. We are probably far too much inclined to over-estimate the conscious character even of intellectual and artistic productions. From the communications of some of the most highly productive persons, such as Goethe and Helmholtz, we learn, indeed, that the most essential and original parts in their creations came to them in the form of inspirations and reached their perceptions almost finished. There is nothing strange about the assistance of the conscious activity in other cases where there was a concerted effort of all the psychic forces. But it is a much abused privilege of the conscious activity that it is allowed to hide from us all other activities wherever it participates.

It will hardly be worth while to take up the historical significance of dreams as a special subject. Where, for instance, a chieftain has been urged through a dream to engage in a bold undertaking the success of which has had the effect of changing history, a new problem results only so long as the dream, regarded as a strange power, is contrasted with other more familiar psychic forces; the problem, however, disappears when we regard the dream as a form

of expression for feelings which are burdened with resistance during the day and which can receive reinforcements at night from deep emotional sources. But the great respect shown by the ancients for the dream is based on a correct psychological surmise. It is a homage paid to the unsubdued and indestructible in the human mind, and to the demoniacal which furnishes the dream-wish and which we find again in our unconscious.

Not inadvisedly do I use the expression "in our unconscious," for what we so designate does not coincide with the unconscious of the philosophers, nor with the unconscious of Lipps. In the latter uses it is intended to designate only the opposite of conscious. That there are also unconscious psychic processes beside the conscious ones is the hotly contested and energetically defended issue. Lipps gives us the more far-reaching theory that everything psychic exists as unconscious, but that some of it may exist also as conscious. But it was not to prove this theory that we have adduced the phenomena of the dream and of the hysterical symptom formation; the observation of normal life alone suffices to establish its correctness beyond any doubt. The new fact that we have learned from the analysis of the psychopathological formations, and indeed from their first member, viz. dreams, is that the unconscious—hence the psychic—occurs as a function of two separate systems and that it occurs as such even in normal psychic life. Consequently there are two kinds of unconscious, which we do not as yet find distinguished by the psychologists. Both are unconscious in the psychological sense; but in our sense the first, which we call Unc., is likewise incapable of consciousness, whereas the second we term "Forec." because its emotions, after the observance of certain rules, can reach consciousness, perhaps not before they have again undergone censorship, but still regardless of the Unc. system. The fact that in order to attain consciousness the emotions must traverse an unalterable series of events or succession of instances, as is betrayed through their alteration by the censor, has helped us to draw a comparison from spatiality. We described the relations of the two systems to each other and to consciousness

by saying that the system Forec. is like a screen between the system Unc. and consciousness. The system Forec. not only bars access to consciousness, but also controls the entrance to voluntary motility and is capable of sending out a sum of mobile energy, a portion of which is familiar to us as attention.

We must also steer clear of the distinctions superconscious and subconscious which have found so much favor in the more recent literature on the psychoneuroses, for just such a distinction seems to emphasize the equivalence of the psychic and the conscious.

What part now remains in our description of the once all-powerful and all-overshadowing consciousness? None other than that of a sensory organ for the perception of psychic qualities. According to the fundamental idea of schematic undertaking we can conceive the conscious perception only as the particular activity of an independent system for which the abbreviated designation "Cons." commends itself. This system we conceive to be similar in its mechanical characteristics to the perception system P, hence excitable by qualities and incapable of retaining the trace of changes, i.e. it is devoid of memory. The psychic apparatus which, with the sensory organs of the P-system, is turned to the outer world, is itself the outer world for the sensory organ of Cons.; the teleological justification of which rests on this relationship. We are here once more confronted with the principle of the succession of instances which seems to dominate the structure of the apparatus. The material under excitement flows to the Cons, sensory organ from two sides, firstly from the P-system whose excitement, qualitatively determined, probably experiences a new elaboration until it comes to conscious perception; and, secondly, from the interior of the apparatus itself, the quantitative processes of which are perceived as a qualitative series of pleasure and pain as soon as they have undergone certain changes.

The philosophers, who have learned that correct and highly complicated thought structures are possible even without the coöperation of consciousness, have found it difficult to attribute any function to consciousness; it has appeared to them a superfluous

mirroring of the perfected psychic process. The analogy of our Cons. system with the systems of perception relieves us of this embarrassment. We see that perception through our sensory organs results in directing the occupation of attention to those paths on which the incoming sensory excitement is diffused; the qualitative excitement of the P-system serves the mobile quantity of the psychic apparatus as a regulator for its discharge. We may claim the same function for the overlying sensory organ of the Cons. system. By assuming new qualities, it furnishes a new contribution toward the guidance and suitable distribution of the mobile occupation quantities. By means of the perceptions of pleasure and pain, it influences the course of the occupations within the psychic apparatus, which normally operates unconsciously and through the displacement of quantities. It is probable that the principle of pain first regulates the displacements of occupation automatically, but it is quite possible that the consciousness of these qualities adds a second and more subtle regulation which may even oppose the first and perfect the working capacity of the apparatus by placing it in a position contrary to its original design for occupying and developing even that which is connected with the liberation of pain. We learn from neuropsychology that an important part in the functional activity of the apparatus is attributed to such regulations through the qualitative excitation of the sensory organs. The automatic control of the primary principle of pain and the restriction of mental capacity connected with it are broken by the sensible regulations, which in their turn are again automatisms. We learn that the repression which, though originally expedient, terminates nevertheless in a harmful rejection of inhibition and of psychic domination, is so much more easily accomplished with reminiscences than with perceptions, because in the former there is no increase in occupation through the excitement of the psychic sensory organs. When an idea to be rejected has once failed to become conscious because it has succumbed to repression, it can be repressed on other occasions only because it has been withdrawn from conscious perception on other grounds. These are hints employed by therapy in order to bring about a retrogression of accomplished repressions.

The value of the over-occupation which is produced by the regulating influence of the Cons. sensory organ on the mobile quantity, is demonstrated in the teleological connection by nothing more clearly than by the creation of a new series of qualities and consequently a new regulation which constitutes the precedence of man over the animals. For the mental processes are in themselves devoid of quality except for the excitements of pleasure and pain accompanying them, which, as we know, are to be held in check as possible disturbances of thought. In order to endow them with a quality, they are associated in man with verbal memories, the qualitative remnants of which suffice to draw upon them the attention of consciousness which in turn endows thought with a new mobile energy.

The manifold problems of consciousness in their entirety can be examined only through an analysis of the hysterical mental process. From this analysis we receive the impression that the transition from the foreconscious to the occupation of consciousness is also connected with a censorship similar to the one between the Unc. and the Forec. This censorship, too, begins to act only with the reaching of a certain quantitative degree, so that few intense thought formations escape it. Every possible case of detention from consciousness, as well as of penetration to consciousness, under restriction is found included within the picture of the psychoneurotic phenomena; every case points to the intimate and twofold connection between the censor and consciousness. I shall conclude these psychological discussions with the report of two such occurrences.

On the occasion of a consultation a few years ago the subject was an intelligent and innocent-looking girl. Her attire was strange; whereas a woman's garb is usually groomed to the last fold, she had one of her stockings hanging down and two of her waist buttons opened. She complained of pains in one of her legs, and exposed her leg unrequested. Her chief complaint, however, was in her own words as follows: She had a feeling in her body as if something was stuck into it which moved to and fro and made her tremble through and through. This sometimes made her whole body stiff. On hearing

this, my colleague in consultation looked at me; the complaint was quite plain to him. To both of us it seemed peculiar that the patient's mother thought nothing of the matter; of course she herself must have been repeatedly in the situation described by her child. As for the girl, she had no idea of the import of her words or she would never have allowed them to pass her lips. Here the censor had been deceived so successfully that under the mask of an innocent complaint a phantasy was admitted to consciousness which otherwise would have remained in the foreconscious.

Another example: I began the psychoanalytic treatment of a boy of fourteen years who was suffering from *tic convulsif*, hysterical vomiting, headache, &c., by assuring him that, after closing his eyes, he would see pictures or have ideas, which I requested him to communicate to me. He answered by describing pictures. The last impression he had received before coming to me was visually revived in his memory. He had played a game of checkers with his uncle, and now saw the checkerboard before him. He commented on various positions that were favorable or unfavorable, on moves that were not safe to make. He then saw a dagger lying on the checker-board, an object belonging to his father, but transferred to the checker-board by his phantasy. Then a sickle was lying on the board; next a scythe was added; and, finally, he beheld the likeness of an old peasant mowing the grass in front of the boy's distant parental home. A few days later I discovered the meaning of this series of pictures. Disagreeable family relations had made the boy nervous. It was the case of a strict and crabbed father who lived unhappily with his mother, and whose educational methods consisted in threats; of the separation of his father from his tender and delicate mother, and the remarrying of his father, who one day brought home a young woman as his new mamma. The illness of the fourteen-year-old boy broke out a few days later. It was the suppressed anger against his father that had composed these pictures into intelligible allusions. The material was furnished by a reminiscence from mythology, The sickle was the one with which Zeus castrated his father; the scythe and the likeness of the peasant represented Kronos, the violent old man who eats his children and

upon whom Zeus wreaks vengeance in so unfilial a manner. The marriage of the father gave the boy an opportunity to return the reproaches and threats of his father—which had previously been made because the child played with his genitals (the checkerboard; the prohibitive moves; the dagger with which a person may be killed). We have here long repressed memories and their unconscious remnants which, under the guise of senseless pictures have slipped into consciousness by devious paths left open to them.

I should then expect to find the theoretical value of the study of dreams in its contribution to psychological knowledge and in its preparation for an understanding of neuroses. Who can foresee the importance of a thorough knowledge of the structure and activities of the psychic apparatus when even our present state of knowledge produces a happy therapeutic influence in the curable forms of the psychoneuroses? What about the practical value of such study some one may ask, for psychic knowledge and for the discovering of the secret peculiarities of individual character? Have not the unconscious feelings revealed by the dream the value of real forces in the psychic life? Should we take lightly the ethical significance of the suppressed wishes which, as they now create dreams, may some day create other things?

I do not feel justified in answering these questions. I have not thought further upon this side of the dream problem. I believe, however, that at all events the Roman Emperor was in the wrong who ordered one of his subjects executed because the latter dreamt that he had killed the Emperor. He should first have endeavored to discover the significance of the dream; most probably it was not what it seemed to be. And even if a dream of different content had the significance of this offense against majesty, it would still have been in place to remember the words of Plato, that the virtuous man contents himself with dreaming that which the wicked man does in actual life. I am therefore of the opinion that it is best to accord freedom to dreams. Whether any reality is to be attributed to the unconscious wishes, and in what sense, I am not prepared to say offhand. Reality must naturally be denied to all transition—and intermediate thoughts. If we had before us the unconscious wishes, brought to their last and

truest expression, we should still do well to remember that more than one single form of existence must be ascribed to the psychic reality. Action and the conscious expression of thought mostly suffice for the practical need of judging a man's character. Action, above all, merits to be placed in the first rank; for many of the impulses penetrating consciousness are neutralized by real forces of the psychic life before they are converted into action; indeed, the reason why they frequently do not encounter any psychic obstacle on their way is because the unconscious is certain of their meeting with resistances later. In any case it is instructive to become familiar with the much raked-up soil from which our virtues proudly arise. For the complication of human character moving dynamically in all directions very rarely accommodates itself to adjustment through a simple alternative, as our antiquated moral philosophy would have it.

And how about the value of the dream for a knowledge of the future? That, of course, we cannot consider. One feels inclined to substitute: "for a knowledge of the past." For the dream originates from the past in every sense. To be sure the ancient belief that the dream reveals the future is not entirely devoid of truth. By representing to us a wish as fulfilled the dream certainly leads us into the future; but this future, taken by the dreamer as present, has been formed into the likeness of that past by the indestructible wish.

◆◆◆